For the Feeling

LOVE &
TRANSFORMATION
FROM NEW YORK
TO CAPE TOWN

Judyie Al-Bilali

Dedicated to
my parents,
Lillian and George Brandt,
who brought me to earth
&
to my children,
Lillian Hanan and Muhammad Salim,
who kept me here

Gratitude

Medi, for being famous

Miki, for being my soul sister

Ingrid, for being my home girl far away from home

Shirley & UWC English Department, for your generosity

Brian & Office of the Rector, for your support

Terry & Augusta Savage Gallery, for your vision

Xavier & Inshaff, for your commitment

Ekophelini Centre, for the beginning

Diana, for making me welcome

Monica, for recognizing my work

Lilyane, for keeping the home fires burning

Liz, for keeping the light on

Mike, for keeping the faith

Susan, for seeing the big picture

Talvin, for being my art brother

Valerie, for dedication to the page

Ruth, for hearing clearly

Ellen, for capturing shadow and sun

Mikey OneSoul, for believing in beauty

Nyatui, for generous tech savvy

Stan, for coaching across the finish line

Liesel, for understanding then and now

My brother, George, for saying "yes"

Shahid, for your devotion to family

Johnette, for being midwife, confidant, cheerleader, champion

and Editor Extraordinaire

Buster, for being there

Diva, for being free

and for all Brown Paper Studio company members

all over the world,

You Know Who You Are

Special Thanks to the Art Angels

friends who generously contributed to the creation of
For the Feeling

Aunt Muriel Lightsy

Frances-Ann Lightsy

Jill Nelson

Rachel & Jack O'Brien

Drew Jaglom

Angel Hardy Heinz

Vicky Stark

Frank "The Terrible" Williams

Michael Lutin

Nyatui Turnage

Penny Remsen

Nick Orsborn

Aishah Rahman

Tom Norton

Deborah Harris

Darnley Beckles

Elizabeth Jackson

Jim McConnell & Joe Hickey

Stanley Nelson

Kanda Gordon

Steve Harnik

Alan Main

Nina Beaty

Janice & Leo Frame

Talvin Wilks

Lello Sekesseke

Theo Phillips

Mike Finn

Richard Friedhoff

Martin Harris

Richard Trousdell

Susan T. MacKenzie

Linda McInerney

Valerie Barker

Yvonne Sanders-Hamilton

Part One

Heart Transplant

Prologue

These are the old days

The words are typed across my mind.

It has happened all my life—I get crystal-clear messages written in courier font on the inside of my skull when it is time to change or relocate or realize something important. The phrase about the "old days" has been appearing since I could recognize language. Intuitively I know it means "pay attention," "take note," "the world won't always be this way and you'll want to remember."

"These are the old days" reminds me that those generations lining up in the ethers for their journey here may not believe me. I can tell the recent arrivals that I lived through it, that I was a pioneer, that I always knew the world would transform into the new earth where we live now, an evolved planet where humans realize we are sovereign beings.

These are the old days.

2001

Across the Threshold
Divorce

"Go live with the dead then. Curl up with a nice pile of—what did they call it? Plexiglas.
Make a little dwelling of the I-beams and rebar. You always loved that shit.
I don't need anyone. . ."

Mama, *So Far*

I
t is cold. Gray. January in New England. We are standing in front
of an imposing concrete building with no windows in Amherst,
Massachusetts. We don't talk, my husband and I. We haven't spoken
in weeks. I have a big round bald spot on the back left side of my head
called alopecia nervosa. Means your nerves are shot and it's causing
your hair to fall out because of the suffocating tension in your home.

We are in the process of a divorce decided on Halloween weekend,
not long after the Twin Towers fell. Since then we've lived in our own
sad, silent war zone, interrupted only by grunts and dismissive gestures.

Daily my husband will come into the house with ice-encrusted boots and lay on the couch where he's been sleeping and watch feature-length animated movies like *101 Dalmatians* and *Feivel Goes West* while his boots drip sooty puddles on the rug.

"He always felt that way about you, it's just now he can show it," blurts out my girlfriend. Was it so obvious? Could everyone predict that my husband would simply stop speaking to me? That he would erase my presence in a room with a disgusted wave of his hand? His tactics are equal parts contempt and heartbreak. I'm supposed to be on my way to South Africa as a visiting artist. I feel so messed up I almost don't go.

A couple of years before our decision to divorce, while in graduate school, I was cast in the play *So Far*. It was a new script by noted dramatist Connie Congdon, a biting, funny, unwieldy production in which I played a madwoman called Mama. She's a narcissistic, postapocalyptic wife who killed her husband by hitting him in the head with a shovel, only to have him rise from the grave at the end of act one. While pretending to be confined to a wheelchair, she "raises" her peculiar children in the aftermath of civilization and keeps an orphaned man-boy as a sex toy. Mama is certified raunchy. This mega manic role was my first time back onstage in almost twenty years, and before I committed to performing in this three-hour epic, I asked Shahid to read the play. I wanted him to give me his opinion and hopefully his blessing. He said, yes, do the show, and no, he will not come to see me. I didn't ask why. I didn't want to be talked out of it. I suspected that watching his wife perform in front of a few hundred people as a wacky, hypersexed, murderous woman was a bit much. I respected his decision, a decision that subconsciously freed me to go to the emotional extremes the role demanded. I also didn't ask why, because whatever the answer, it was the first red flag of our impending separation. I knew that just like Mama's husband, once my buried actor was resurrected from her tomb, there was no way she would ever go underground again.

"Somewhere deep inside, swimming in this bile, foul with memory and hatred, there's a molecule of—love may be too strong a word: 'affection' maybe 'habit'. We're hard-wired to love."

Mama, *So Far*

The bus arrives. My husband asks the driver if it's going to New York. Then this man who is the father of my children, who stood by me through a devastating bout with cancer, who has been my best friend for much of my adult life, sets down my suitcase, turns, and walks away without a word. I am stunned. Embarrassed. I call out his name.

"Shahid?"

My questioning voice is feeble. It's a pathetic attempt to at least look normal. My husband keeps walking, each step a plodding resolution to leave me behind. Rage rolls off his back like steam in the frozen air. The most dangerous cold on this wintery day is between us.

What was my question going to be? *Are you the man I married? Am I the woman you loved?* As I step up onto the bus, I realize I have just gotten divorced. It's not about courts or custody or lawyers. In this frigid, empty moment, my marriage of eighteen years is done. "Goodbye, Shahid," I say to no one, and I lift my other foot across the threshold to a new life.

𝔎

A little Colored baby, a Negro girl, someday a Black teenager, and
ultimately a grown-up African American woman arrives on the edge
of one era crashing into the next. School integration is around the
corner when I land in this fragile, brown, female body; born in Harlem
to devoted working-class parents, light-skinned Race people who
covet the American Dream in all its contradictions. I have a brother
older by ten years who resents me from the word go. It takes a while
for him to forgive me for coming into the world, for disturbing his
exclusive only-child status.

I love animals, and my sentimental heart is nurtured in the embrace
of our pets: several rescued dogs, two guinea pigs, and a turtle. School
is rich, white, and downtown. Park Avenue and penthouses. Home is
uptown, 135th Street between Lenox and Fifth Avenue. Harlem Hospital
and the Schomburg Centre for Research in Black Culture. In school I
am smart in everything except math. I have to be smart, because I am
on a scholarship and I Am Different. Despite my otherness, by junior
high school I start to see myself as a desirable female. Boys like me. I like
them. I fall in love at thirteen at a backyard summer party on Martha's
Vineyard, and at sixteen follow him to Chicago after wrangling my way
out of high school a year before graduation.

Following Love is the story of my life.

Between working as an actor and dancer, I study at five assorted
colleges and universities, finally graduating with a self-designed degree
in African American Performing Arts. All my back-and-forth, up-and-
down with higher education confirms what I already know—that I am
an artist and I have real talent. If I want something—a role, a boyfriend,

an opportunity—I get it. I sail along assuredly full of myself, realizing I'm a change agent.

Anywhere I go will be different after I leave.

I am hired for shows in Texas and Massachusetts and New York, and somewhere in my midtwenties, I have an affair with a big, charismatic married man who is destined to someday become a star on TV. He dumps me, and my shattered confidence as a woman and performer haunts me for the next twenty years.

I marry Shahid, a brilliant, self-educated man, a bona fide genius, and my finest artistic collaborator. From our first kiss, I confirm what science has finally proven: women know instantly from deep within our genetic codes who will be a suitable father for our children. Although he and I love each other profoundly, we are never truly lovers. We are genuinely caring parents to two remarkable human beings. Our kids are gifted, conscious, occasional pains-in-the-ass, and highly evolved. They will keep me on earth when illness almost convinces me to die. For them, I am eternally grateful.

After "Goodbye, Shahid," I fly to South Africa to discover that I am an exceptional teacher. I fall in love with a former student; a man half my age. Quite abruptly I get clobbered. I get up and dust myself off. From now on I will *allow* myself to be in love, I'm done with falling.

My recovery from the blow of being a jilted older woman unwittingly sparks what will become my creative process,, a synthesis of What I Know. I've made it to this moment in time and space when my 1960s adolescent dreams of peace and love are all about to come true. Somehow I persist in believing that this planet is a glorious place. I manage to trust myself enough to figure out a method for others to trust themselves in preparation for life on the new earth we inhabit.

I call my method Brown Paper Studio.

It has already changed the world.

2002

In Our Lifetime
Identity

Journal Entry, Johannesburg
Images of wealth and privilege. . .images of destitution and despair. . .the brain bleeds in
an effort to reconcile these realities.

I have to make fun of myself learning Zulu words. I sound like Daffy Duck. My
pronunciation makes everyone laugh, and they end up saying just call me Bani or Loki
or something equally simple for an American whose names are Bob or Kate. This next
phase of my life really must include learning another language.

"**M**y name is Zoeleka. I will be your interpreter."
A small, stout woman, in the characteristic beret worn
all year long by South African women, greets me warmly. Her hat is
mustard yellow and her brown cheeks are round as sunrise. I am preparing to conduct a theater workshop at Ekophelini Mental Health
Centre. Ekophelini means Place of Hope, and as I will discover on my
first day of teaching in South Africa, the name is an apt description. I

am in the country for one month as a visiting artist from the Augusta Savage Gallery at the University of Massachusetts. I've been chosen to inaugurate the International Artist Exchange Program, with my first week in Johannesburg and the remaining time in Cape Town. I am here to facilitate theater workshops for youth and adults.

The Exchange Program is the creation of my longtime friend and artistic collaborator, Terry, the gallery director. We met in our twenties, young women with big Afros and big ideas. We have been art sisters for over thirty years. After Terry's visit to South Africa in 2001, she decided to offer other performing and visual artists the opportunity to experience living abroad for a month. One is free to work, rest, research, sightsee, read, sleep, whatever cultivates the creative spirit. The only requirement after our sojourn is to perform or exhibit in her gallery's next season. Quite a gift.

Ekophelini, a government-sponsored mental health clinic, is my host for this first day of workshops. The clinic trains community people as mental health facilitators in an innovative system of satellite support groups. It is a small facility, serving the mental health needs of more than ten thousand people, any of whom could justifiably describe themselves on any given day as being completely emotionally traumatized by the conditions of their life. East Rand is notorious for extreme overcrowding and violent crime. The living conditions are deplorable. People live in shacks, most without windows and floors, and none that I visited had indoor plumbing. One outside faucet serves more than a hundred people's need for water. There are a few dilapidated portable toilets. Dwellings are unheated, and South African winters are cold. Even according to the official census, the unemployment rate averages around 70 percent. Those who can afford it have electricity in their shacks, an expensive luxury offering township residents the chance to become hypnotized by television and its distant glossy world that wants to forget them. Today's schedule is trial by fire. As I wait in the cinderblock building's reception area, I feel slightly overwhelmed. I ask myself, "What could I possibly offer in one day?" The essentials of what I have learned in three decades as a theater artist will be distilled into these few hours on the outskirts of Johannesburg.

Playing close by on one of the gray metal chairs is a little girl of four years wearing an oversized white hospital gown and holding on tight to a teddy bear. Someone has lovingly fixed her hair in braids with fat curly ringlets at the end. Underneath the loose gown is a wide bandage. She was bitten in the stomach by a person possessed by evil spirits. It is an unthinkable act. As the mind recoils, it also registers that the level of rage people here must endure daily is equally incomprehensible. The child walks barefoot around the clinic, feeling comfortable enough to climb up on a chair and introduce me to her stuffed toy.

My first session is a bereavement group for people with AIDS and people who are HIV positive. The participants are in various stages of health and illness, some moving with obvious pain and difficulty. Singing begins every meeting at Ekophelini. Many meetings in South Africa traditionally start with raising voices together. Today's song is for a group member's relative who passed away in the previous week. Death is a frequent visitor, funerals punctuate everyone's life in this sprawling township of over one hundred thousand people.

Once the opening song establishes harmony and resonance in the room, I am introduced as a guest artist for the day. I always begin by having us stand in a circle to offer an expression of gratitude, to state our collective creative intent. We play games to get us laughing, conduct exercises to get us moving, and pose questions to get us communicating. Zoeleka turns my English into Zulu, her excellent translation evoking immediate response from the participants, who even think my jokes are funny.

At the start of sessions, most people stand contracted, their shoulders tight, their breathing shallow. They don't know what to expect. They don't know that laughing and looking silly is encouraged. Because I'm acting a clown, making faces, strange sounds, and big broad raucous movements, slowly they start to unwind. When I work with adults, the first movements in games are tiny and tentative. Politely they make hand gestures and timid noises. This work is unfamiliar, and they avoid using the lower part of their bodies—their hips and thighs and knees and groin and butt. I work hard to unlock and encourage these bodies, always by demonstrating with my own. I work hard to make them smile. The atmosphere of the room lightens in the warm-up.

"She looks like she has lost something."

"…her friend."

"Oh, very sad. She has been crying."

"…or a baby, maybe she lost a baby."

"Then she would be down on her knees."

We are listening to participants—or actors, as I address them during today's workshop— comment on the human statues standing motionless in the room. They have sculpted the frozen postures on the bodies of their fellow actors. I am conducting a variation on the Modeling Exercise of master theater artist Augusto Boal. Actors form two lines facing each other; one side becomes the sculptors and the other side the statues. In silent pairs, they manipulate their partner's body, even facial expressions, into an image of the emotion that I prompt. Grief, joy, surprise, anger, pleasure are all expressed. The tremendous range of human emotion is visible in the wide variety of interpretations. Together the sculptors verbally reflect on what they see in the statues. For the next round, roles are reversed between sculptor and statue.

"This one, he has just won the lottery."

"...and a car...a *new* car. Look at his face!"

"With a new girlfriend to drive around!"

The candid responses bring on hilarity. The room swells with confidence, and at the same time, the concentration required invokes an atmosphere of intimacy. It is the body that must be freed. The body is where the traumas are trapped, whether racism or poverty or sexual abuse. The body's release opens the eyes, the windows to the soul, and by the end of a session, many eyes are sparkling. I am thanked graciously, asked when I am coming back. I explain I am only there for the day, though somewhere in my bones, I know that I am hooked. My life has taken a new turn.

Quietly observing is Johanna, the director of Ekophelini. She is the mother of several adopted daughters from infant to teen and each with their own health challenges. She is tall, blond, and from Botswana. To say Johanna works tirelessly is a gross understatement. She notices approvingly that the group was particularly animated and that it is unusual for people to move and touch so freely. There is reluctance about physical contact because of the nature of the disease. Touch is so vital to my process, I never thought about not being physically close. I recognize how ignorant I am and thankful I did not blunder.

The boys' group at Ekophelini meets immediately after the bereavement group. It is a group of eight, all on the verge of being young men. They gather every week to support each other for the singular and courageous act of staying out of a gang. I engage the boys in one of my favorite warm-ups, the Animal Game. Like most theater games, the Animal Game begins in a circle. Each player chooses an animal and creates a corresponding gesture. We go around the circle to memorize everyone's animal and movement. One player stands in the center and calls out any player's animal while making the gesture. Right away that person must say the name of his animal, make his gesture, then quickly call out someone else's animal and make his gesture. That next player picks it up and so on, until the one in the middle is fast enough to tag someone. Once a player is tagged, he is in the middle and the game begins again. It goes fast, and invariably the whole thing gets ridiculous as people are mixing up animals and gestures and falling down giddy. It takes a while to catch on, and when the boys get the hang of it, they don't want to stop. They are children, and it has been a long time since they have just played.

After the games, Johanna opens the weekly discussion. A boy of slight build with plaintive eyes confides to this group that he's proud to be a good student. He is homeless, living in a storage room in the back of a *shabeen*, one of the countless makeshift taverns found in every township. He wants to read at night, but the uproar of the drunken patrons disturbs him. They are constantly fighting. He cannot concentrate. He breaks down crying in frustration. Johanna suggests that a shed on the side of the clinic building could become a study hall. The youth would have to clean it up and maintain it so they could have a quiet space for learning. His tears are eased. Place of Hope is well named.

Journal Entry, Cape Town
Sitting in the bright morning kitchen, the sun on my back, I hope the heat will grow hair on the naked patch of my scalp. Last night we ate a late South African dinner, lamb cooked Xhosa-style, vegetables, potatoes, bread, salad, chocolate mousse, and red wine. Whenever you eat here, you think of the closeness of devastating hunger. Distributing the food yesterday to the children—their urgency could be felt as they held out their hands for apples. Their grasp was not sure when the next apple would arrive.

"Look, but don't touch."

This is what Ingrid warns, watching my pupils dilate for a gorgeous young Black African student. He's from Angola, in his twenties having come to South Africa awhile ago as an "unaccompanied minor." Ingrid and I, mutual friends of Terry, have been working diligently on our production of *What I Want You to Know* for ten days. He pops up on my radar as we're running our final dress and tech rehearsal at Guga S'Thebe Community Centre. He is a featured musician playing excellent guitar. I'm well over forty and startled by my own fantasies. Ingrid is right, hands off.

Ingrid and I are bosom buddies from the States. We share a taste for fine Black men, wine, food, music, parties, art, laughter, and South

Africa. Ingrid is tall, with topaz eyes and a regal style. Her skin is Lindt dark chocolate. Her hospitality is legendary. She has been living in Cape Town for a couple of years and has arranged our three-week theater project. Ingrid was one of the directors of the Interfaith Pilgrimage, an enormous undertaking that organized a group of Buddhist monks and lay people of all descriptions to retrace the route of the Middle Passage from Africa through the New World—on foot, no less. The journey took almost two years. I tease Ingrid that she's a different kind of sister, ringing bells and chanting and walking across half the earth. Her projects are always ambitious, so why am I not surprised when she tells me that we have ten days to create an original theater piece with a group of twenty-eight young people from South Africa, Angola, Burundi, Congo, Rwanda, and Nigeria. All the non-South African students are refugees. They range in age from eight to twenty-four years. Minimal English is the common language. When I'm teaching, students will listen intently and nod, not having the slightest idea of what I'm talking about. I'll ask someone more fluent if the others understand what I'm saying.

"No, they just like your American accent. It sounds like television."

There will be many instances when my nasal twang of cultural imperialism lets me "win friends and influence people." It's a paradox I learn to accept.

Journal Entry, Cape Town

The work is going well. It is incredibly demanding. I can feel the strain in my lower back and legs. I am tired and wired. I was so pleased today when our script was complete. We finally had a full run-through. They are learning a lot in a short time, and so am I. Our piece is beautiful. It says something. It means something.

On the second day of rehearsal, I notice that by eleven in the morning, no one can concentrate. The room is spaced out, lethargic. It occurs to me that very few of these young actors had breakfast and some perhaps not much dinner. I make arrangements to feed the entire company for the remainder of the project. My philanthropy costs all of one hundred dollars. I wonder, as I will countless times in the coming years, what kind of world is this where it is so simple to care for people and still we cannot provide basic human needs?

Our show at Guga S'Thebe is a hit. We perform on a small amphitheater stage in an artful, well-designed community center complex. We get a standing ovation from the outdoor benches filled with township residents and invited guests. Children from the audience run up onstage and dance gaily to the post-show music. The eruption of joy backstage is like nothing I have ever seen in my decades of theater. Our newly formed pan-African company of actors and musicians is shouting and laughing and hugging and crying. I've worked nonstop for ten days, my molecules feel like they are breaking apart, I am so exhausted I feel transparent. The company's elation is contagious. Despite being bone tired, my mood is one of complete and utter satisfaction.

The title of the show, *What I Want You to Know,* came to me weeks before arriving in Cape Town, prompted by a series of chilling xenophobic attacks by South African citizens on foreign nationals seeking asylum from conflict zones. Ingrid asked me to address the crisis in our production. The plot is simple, one I'll use again working with African youth. We start the play introducing divisions imposed by society that separate the young people and prevent them from enjoying life to the fullest; the instances of prejudice are monotonous and deadening. Despite these barriers, a love interest is ignited, and the romance inspires an exchange of traditional and contemporary songs and dances. Creativity fosters understanding, and the experience of Art brings them to Unity.

While staging the big finale, I set my sights on the Angolan guitar player. Ingrid admonishes me to act my age. I'm leaving in two days anyway, time for me to get on a plane back to New York, so I'm not tempted toward indiscretion. Two months later I get a letter from him. As a result of our show, he was invited to audition at a major university and has received a bursary to study music. Because of our production, his life is totally changed. He moves from the group hostel to campus housing to begin his academic career. In the letter he explains he needs money for food. It is exam time, a grueling period for South African students, since most of their final grade is contingent on test results. He's running on empty and requests my help. I am touched. I am more than touched. I am titillated. I agree to send him some money.

Fast forward. We're now communicating regularly via e-mail, and the messages are getting overheated.

I flirt:

Last night I wrote in my journal to you instead of on the computer and then sent an urgent message to the Full Moon for you to contact me. Again you have the best ears, the moon must've told you I was waiting. She was a big golden summer moon for me, maybe a pale winter moon for you, still she shines the same lovely light on both of us.

He says:

My heart is jumping with joy as I read your e-mail. I'm beginning to find out that somehow, somewhere we (me & you) have things in common. You are romantic too!! It's a pleasure to me to know that my e-mail touches somehow, somewhere your heart.

I'm worse than a teenager. I'm a lonely divorcée who is creating an online romantic persona. I'm eagerly fundraising for a fantasy lover. The Internet is tricky and I'm in a trick bag.

I confess:

Right before everyone went onstage, I walked down the line to wish the company a great show. I placed my hands on people's faces and smiled at them. Halfway down the line, I realized I would have to hold your face in my hands and if I did, you (and maybe others) might sense how I feel about you. That my gesture was not the way a teacher cares for a student, it is the way a woman cares for a man. So then I just put my hands close to everyone's face as I wished them well. When I got to you, my fingertips did not touch you. I made sure not to linger too long in your eyes. I did not wish to embarrass you or myself. I felt that I was too much older than you to have such feelings.

He says:

You are the best, caring, loving and very sweetie woman!! I can feel how happy you are! It makes me happy to! You really make me speechless! My question is: why didn't you speak up the way you feel about me long ago? I suppose you suffered a lot keeping that strong feeling inside. I believe you are feeling much better now. Like I told you, you do not need to keep anything else! Take everything off your heart and expose it to me.

Faster forward. We're talking on the phone, no simple feat given the quality of cell-phone reception plus the language difference.

"Hi…Hello." American greeting.

"Allo…Allo?" Angolan reply.

"Hi. Can you hear me?"

"Allo. I hear you."

"What? Hi."

"Yes."

"What?"

"Allo?"

My life pretty much revolves around these incoherent conversations. Things are getting X-rated online. I sign my messages "Sugar."

I seduce:

You want to hear more pillow talk? Sometimes you're on top, and I can look up and see that beautiful smile, sometimes I'm on top and can snuggle my nose against your neck, sometimes I'm in back to whisper in your ear while I hold you tight, and sometimes you're in back, your hands everywhere and your lips on my shoulders. . .our eyes say everything—fluent in every language. Sometimes we lie side-by-side, stare at the ceiling, and laugh out loud. And sometimes we even sleep. You are so right to be inspired, I do mean every word I write. . .and more. I truly enjoy stroking your ego and that's not all I like to stroke. It's the best I can do in a long-distance telephone relationship, I can stroke pretty well with my words...

He says:

You see Sugar J, in the past few days I've been thinking about "us" and I think that we can make it work, how? I do not know but I'm beginning to believe the love conquers all. I need you to believe it with me.

Speed-dial forward. I'm feverishly planning to visit Cape Town in January to see my paramour. I'm officially calling it a sabbatical. A sabbatical from what? Not having sex?

I surrender:

You want me to call you at nine a.m.? That means I must stay awake until three a.m. Do you think I will? You know I will. Just to hear you call me Baby and Sweetie.

He says:

I'm just realizing that the days are very much close for us to see each other face to face! I can't wait for that moment! In a few days time it's finally going to happen.

I am scheduled to arrive right after the New Year. He and his brother will pick me up at the airport. It's finally going to happen.

Journal Entry, New York

I am shocked having women tell me that they have not been made love to for years—five years, seven years, twelve years. Beautiful, vital women in their 40s, 50s, suffocating in marriages without sex. . .I cannot imagine. . .this is huge. This is a revolution. Women are ashamed, afraid to break their silence. To say anything is to be a castrating bitch. No wonder we're on antidepressants en masse. My therapist suggested I write a play about divorce. That didn't sound too interesting until I started hearing their stories. He must hear them all the time and know there is a mighty dam about to burst. "Sexual neglect" is what I'm calling it. It's rampant. Never mind being called a "crone"—sounds like some dried-up hag from the Middle Ages. It'll be a long time before I answer to that name.

It seems that all my "names" are up for grabs, self-definition at midlife is in flux around both sex and race. Growing up in North America, I thought I had mastered the dance of shifting identity. In South Africa, it seems, I must learn some new steps. I call myself a Black person. I look like a Coloured person. I live like a White person.

One of my students questions me directly:

"Would you really be Black in the United States?"

Her lovely appearance is a startling, unexpected South African mix of diverse and beautiful bloodlines. She identifies as Coloured and imagines I might do the same.

"Oh yes, my dear" I confirm "and so would you."

The first play I wrote was *The Death of Black & White*. It is an allegorical one-act with music and dance about the release of Nelson Mandela from prison at the downfall of apartheid. I figured out the best way for me to get my work produced was to do it myself, so while I was pregnant with our son, Muhammad Salim, Shahid and I premiered the show in 1986. We toured it to the 1987 Women in Theatre Festival, and by that time I was used to hearing comments like "What an inspiring message! What an uplifting show! Too bad it won't happen in our lifetime." Three years later Mandela walked out of prison and into the arms of a jubilant world.

So much will happen in our lifetime.

Creativity will replace productivity as the criteria for success. Instead of being manipulated by the marketplace machine's overdrive hologram, we will live from the inside out, live from the recognition of wholeness and a desire for communion.

After five centuries of global domination by the West, it appeared that gluttonous comfort and slothful convenience were going to triumph as the "Meaning of Life," even if that required desecrating the planet. In this next phase of human evolution, where our survival as a species demands a balance of all hemispheres, East and West, North and South—metaphors for both sides of the brain—integrity will become the priority. Just as in the movie *The Matrix*, collectively we have taken the red pill. We have opted to wake up.

As humanity we were trained away from ourselves. We were taught to want salvation and/or status, to expect something outside of ourselves to raise us up. We were willing to sell our life force in pursuit of "security" from either false gods or governments. Big Daddy is bogus. There are no safe places for anyone, anywhere, if you can't accept yourself. Mass unconsciousness in the form of media mind control will be rendered impotent once you embrace yourself in all your glory—fears and courage and farts and talents and scars and genius and soft spots and raw edges. The task for all of us is about fully accepting the self.

In the blink of an eye, social networking has made us an international community. Rather than pressure us to go impossibly faster, our rapidly advancing technology can provide us true leisure and greater opportunity to slow down, play, reflect, share, and exchange—in person. We need intentional transformational spaces, real-time creative laboratories to practice global citizen skills. More than ever, we crave physical spaces to be human together. More than ever we yearn to know each other, touch each other, laugh and eat and cry and move together. It's not an either-or situation. Technology is not going to wait. Neither is our need for connection.

The young democracy of the New South Africa had awakened a sense of possibility in me. Although the exact language and definitions were still at the conceptual level, this fertile soil was a womb. I had begun gestating a human-centered value system expressed through creativity. A marketing executive prods me: "Can you describe what you do in a sentence?" It will take years of working assiduously and a whole lot of trial and error to formulate my one-liner: "Connect people first to themselves and then to each other."

Journal Entry, New York

This morning my daughter put her arms around me and hugged me and kissed me. "I love you, Mommy," she said. "I know it's hard now, you're just going through a transition. Everything will be all right." All my life I have wanted someone to tell me everything would be all right. That someone turns out to be my daughter.

Back in the States, it's evident to everyone I have left part of myself on the other side of the Atlantic. My family senses my distraction. I am captivated by the frontier of the New South Africa. I quit my university teaching job, move my son from Massachusetts to join his sister in New York, finalize my divorce, lose weight. For the next seven years, my body clock never quite returns to normal. I face East in anticipation of what's ahead.

2003

Be On Time
Lineage

Journal Entry, Cape Town
I thought about suicide yesterday. Being found in my apartment in black lace underwear covered in blood with my wrists slashed...I thought about it for a minute.

From this place of despair, Brown Paper Studio will emerge. It is not born of an academic theory or an artistic notion of community building. It is my lifesaving visceral response to so much loss—the most crucial being that of feeling beautiful, desired, attractive, feminine. I did want to kill myself, or at least disappear off the planet in the absence of tenderness. I scrawled my feelings across brown paper walls to keep from going mad.

I'm getting ahead of myself.

Another January, a new year, a new life, a new love. I have rented #22 Montreux, a comfy one-bedroom apartment in Cape Town, packed my bags, and boarded a plane to travel six thousand miles. My cyberspace lover boy is there as I land on schedule. His head is bobbing up over the crowd in search of me. Have you ever seen the expression on someone's face as they witness a car wreck? That's the face he registers for a nanosecond until he composes himself and plasters a smile across his juicy lips to greet me. His welcome is kind enough, although I've seen the appalled look; already we are topsy-turvy. Apparently I am not who or what he expected, undoubtedly he remembers a younger woman. We are awkward and too polite and in for a very bumpy ride.

Dear Sisters,

No news is good news, so the rapid fire of this e-mail lets you know there's Trouble in Paradise. Well, I predicted there would be some "gates to go through," so from now on, remind me to keep my big, fat, prophetic mouth shut.

The trip began auspiciously enough with your girl getting an upgrade to business class and having an infinitely more enjoyable sixteen-hour plane ride than usual. I was flying with the International Methodist Women's Convention, upwards of one hundred highly motivated postmenopausal Black church sisters strong. I thought to myself as we deplane in Cape Town, I guess he's wondering, "Which one of these old biddies is mine?"

Keep laughing, it gets better.

Your Girl

It wasn't funny. My first line of defense is my girlfriends, my Dear Sisters on the other side of the ocean. Daily, sometimes twice a day, I walk around the corner to the Internet café to pour my pain into the keyboard. Here I am on the other side of the world, unseduced and abandoned. I consider going home. To what? Frozen New York and humiliation? I must stay.

Dear Sisters,

Suffice to say that I've found my niche as a fiction writer because I damn sure made this shit up. As you know, he insisted, long before my arrival, that our relationship remain a secret. I'm still not having it. On my first night in Cape Town, I'm holding tough in my corner and he's firm in his. Round One ends as he crashes off to sleep and I'm left with crazy jet lag, so I unpack, rearrange the apartment, write in my journal, and read two-thirds of a Walter Mosley novel until the sun comes up. In the morning we resume this tedious conversation.

So dig, I'm starting to soften and say what the fuck (literally) and figure, "Hey, I'm here, let's do this, secret or no secret," only to discover that boyfriend has a new girlfriend he met in November! Now I KNOW I asked him on the phone if he was seeing someone, although he says—are you ready, Sisters?

"I don't remember that."

All the progressive crap I ran about "you can have other relationships" sounds worse than a talk-show psychologist. The girlfriend is currently not in town, so he has no qualms about our secret affair. He's managed to be honest and dishonest at the same time.

How do men do that?

Sugar Baby is a TV addict, and since I loathe television, I'm now at the Internet café because he's watching All My Children *and* The Bold and the Beautiful. *Who'd a thunk I was writing a comedy?*

Your Girl

In the midst of it all, Cape Town is even more breathtaking than I remember. I stumble around this most romantic of cities in the blaze of high summer, convinced that everyone can see my shame. Did I mention that over the course of the past year, I not only raised money for his tuition, I bought him a watch, a stereo system, and, in anticipation of our lust-filled holiday, a used car? Considering these substantial investments, I make a decision.

Dear Sisters,

Do you have a copy of Dinah Washington singing "What a Difference a Day Makes"? Play it while you read this e-mail because I broke the fever, by what? Doing the Deed, the Wild Thing, Getting Down, Knocking Boots, all of the above. I had a talk with the angels and they said, "Walk past your own outdated rules and boundaries, love the one you're with." So what if I'm a secret? Get Some. The image I have of these past four turbulent days is how a space shuttle must deal with that incredible fire and noise and speed when breaking through into new atmosphere. Thank you for being Cape Kennedy.

Your Girl

ps

I asked him about his hard-core TV habit, and he told me that's how he taught himself English and was able to excel at the university. I smiled at the irony of "TV as a Second Language" and realize that what you think is mediocrity may be genius if you pause and look a little closer.

Let me give this man some credit, he is not a complete chump and neither am I. He is an absolutely stellar student and maintains a place at the top of the Dean's List throughout his academic career. His only subject with a low mark was the one requiring the stereo system tape player that I self-righteously repossessed in my scorned woman's fury.

"Do you want sex?" he asks me. I've had people offer a cup of coffee with more feeling. What we do is definitely not lovemaking. After the fact, he gets out of bed to remove the condom, and now it's my turn for the auto-wreck face. As he walks to the bathroom, I see that his shoulders are slight, and there is no weight to his step, no heft, no gravitas. His maleness has not yet grounded. I sigh, roll over, and before snoring, mutter the classic phrase, "What was I thinking?" I suppose this tawdry episode is part of him becoming a man and me becoming an older woman. As reported to my girlfriends, I had broken the fever, but I was even more unsatisfied.

Dear Sisters,

Are you both tired of me? Feel free to say, "Follow your heart, continue to risk, break the rules of engagement," or "Bitch, snap out of it and ditch the fool." I think a breakthrough is coming and want to believe if we see each other and have good times, we may find a closer relationship.

Did I just say that? How pathetic! I have to convince someone to want me! Obviously he's got me going in circles (as the classic soul-oldie goes) and I NEED HELP!! I'm counting on you to "Make It Plain," as El Hajj Malik El Shabazz was fond of saying.

Your Girl

I hit send on this slightly hysterical missive and nothing happens. I look up to the counter at the Internet café and anxiously ask a young Black man in dreads, "Do you work here? Can you help me?"

He smiles a radiant smile. "I don't work here, but I can help you." Truer words are rarely spoken. His comeback makes me laugh. I pause, breathe, and consider that perhaps my pushy American panic button is unnecessary. While we wait for the clerk's attention, he proudly shows me his resume.

"I play football. I am Medi. I am a soccer player."

"Are you good?"

An unequivocal "yes."

"Really good?"

I can't resist being pushy. I can't resist that smile.

"Yes," he repeats, squaring his shoulders with an attitude that says, *I told you, of course I am really good.*

Later that evening I will write about him and say there was "not much chemistry" between us. I am ignorant of who this quiet, unassuming man will become to me while I navigate what it means to be an African American in Africa.

Journal Entry, Cape Town

This fabulous thing happens every night after sunset for ten or fifteen minutes. The sky turns royal blue, the mountain slate gray covered by the ethereal "tablecloth" of rolling mist. Buildings glow reflected white. Electric lights are jewels and stars and every other cliché about lights at dusk. The wind is gaining power and the city is magic.

My apartment is absolutely bare. I take down the calendar, hide the only clock in the kitchen cupboard. I need to be without time and schedule. Medi arrives day after day and night after night until I am whole enough to walk to the stationery store to buy a sheet of brown paper and some colored markers. He helps me put the paper up in my bedroom. I prompt him to write something. He is shy, scribbling "Medi bonjour" on the corner piece of masking tape. He pronounces my name with a velvety French *j*, the accent on the second syllable. I don't ask about his age and he doesn't ask about mine. It only comes up when I need to read something and he quips, "You must go get your glasses." I glare at his sideswipe. One day I see his passport and gasp. I'm disgusted with myself. "No, no," he assures me with a laugh, "athletes are always young on paper." It's easier to believe him than question my sanity.

Dodo Cardoso Santos Medi, the magnificent midfielder from the Democratic Republic of Congo living in South Africa as a refugee, courts me. Patiently. Sweetly. He does not understand my impulsiveness, my sobbing, my sadness. I cannot discuss my other infatuation or the betrayal. He doesn't ask. Although he knows there is someone else, he is not deterred. He does not question my moods, he is simply present. His lack of judgment gives me the stability to write every day in my journals, on computers at the Internet café, and on my brown paper wall. Whatever our differences in age, culture, religion, background, and language, both of us are seeking refuge, him from a civil war fueled by multinational greed and aggression, me from stateside consumer greed and apathy. "Not much chemistry" becomes love.

Brown paper goes up to catch my bloody, exploding, splattered heart. The pages of my journal are not big enough. A computer screen can hardly contain my intensity. I need full-body writing. In the passionate hot weather, I am driven by the big, blank, brown canvas. I take off most of my clothes, grab a marker, and start writing. I play loud music. I draw pictures. I laugh and I cry at my heart and my mind taking shape on the paper. The paper fills up fast.

I put another piece up in my bedroom and one in the hallway for guests. I start doing workshops in my house with the students I taught last year, the same young people from all around the continent who created *What I Want You to Know*. We sing and play theater games and eat. I invite them to write on the brown paper walls. They write alone and together, creating poetry and graffiti tags. On the wall their ideas are coming out in a more expansive way than on the page, the writing is personal and public. It is a different wave of expression, bigger, more colorful. Everyone likes to write on the wall precisely because you're not supposed to, what you were forbidden to do as a kid is now encouraged.

People are liberated when given permission to draw or scribble together, their child comes out to play. It's graffiti, cave art, hieroglyphics. It's communal. It's the individual and the collective—me alongside you.

Brown Paper has been informed by an extraordinary lineage of teachers. They are black, white, gay, lesbian, and straight. They are the best, and they insist that I do my best. I began my performance career early by imitating TV commercials and dancing along with *American Bandstand.* "Put that girl in acting classes," my Aunt Sissie advises after she sees me deftly imitate the dog, Farfel, on the Nestlé's cocoa ad. It's not until tenth grade that I start my theater training at The Dalton School on the posh Upper East Side.

It is the 1960s, and Dalton has a reputation for being a liberal, progressive institution. I'm strolling down Madison Avenue on my way to rehearsal for our high school production of a play by e.e. cummings—no schmaltzy musicals for us. I stop in front of a shop window, entranced by the exotica. In the psychedelic '60s, all kinds of fascinating paraphernalia are starting to appear: fabric from India, golden meditation bells from Tibet, black lights, and lava lamps. Rehearsal starts in five minutes, and if I keep walking, I'll just make it on time. I decide to linger and smell the oils and admire the tie-dyed outfits and buy a few sticks of sandalwood incense. I mean, after all, I'm the star of the show and not much can happen without me. I figure I'll be there soon enough. More than half an hour later, I walk into rehearsal. My very first teacher of theater, Miss Ann MacKay, is standing at the auditorium door. She is wearing her standard flat loafer shoes and tweed skirt, her hair cut short with bangs. Her usually genial voice rings harsh:

"You are very late. You have kept us all waiting. Who do you think you are?"

Who do I think I am? I think I am getting my ass handed to me. The rest of the cast is looking and not looking, the way people do when a scene gets embarrassing. Miss MacKay is my favorite teacher. I am one of her favorite students. She has cast me in the plum role of this poetic, offbeat play. I have betrayed the company by letting my head get puffed. I am chagrined at my fall from grace. I want my teacher to be proud of me. Miss MacKay lives in walking distance from school with her partner, Miss Losse, and once a year the theater class is invited over for a social afternoon at their house. I love that she invites us into their home—not many teachers do, and certainly not a female teacher who lives with her female lover. During an annual visit on the way to use the bathroom, I walked past their bedroom with its neatly made double bed. I marvel that someone could be so open with the truth about themselves. It makes me want to be open and true, too. Would I ever again be invited over with the rest of the class to visit that special place?

Being chastised by Miss MacKay taught me one of my most important lessons in theater: we are part of a whole, we are responsible to each other, so-called stars must work harder than anyone else, the company must be respected. It is the collective effort that lets us all shine. Years later as an adult actor, I would work with a top-notch stage manager who announces on the first day of every show:

"We are now on Theater Time. If you are five minutes late, it's multiplied by everyone in the room, cast, crew, designers—twelve people times five minutes is an hour of creative time. Don't be late."

I didn't fall from grace that day. I was initiated into "a life in the theater." After all was said and done, I was still one of my teacher's favorites. From Miss Ann MacKay, I learned what would become the foundation principle of Brown Paper Studio: Be On Time.

From Professor Archie Shepp, prolific composer and stellar musician, I learned the language of Black music. I learned about the unbroken continuum from field holler to blues shout to jazz, gospel, R&B, Hip Hop, and beyond. I learned about the primacy of call and response. I learned about spirit possession, how other dimensions can experience us and we can experience them through music. In Professor Shepp's scholarship, these are "revolutionary concepts in African American music," the title of this most popular undergraduate class at UMass Amherst. He made sure we understood that Black music has nonstop reinvented, reinvigorated, and economically resuscitated American culture since Africans arrived in the West. Studying with him gave me the historical references to define the infusion of Black music into my work as an actor, a director, a playwright, and a teacher. I learned that I am moving the continuum forward.

From Professor Virginia Scott, I learned precision in language and dramaturgical research. Virginia's infamous razor-sharp tongue caught me unaware in her first-year graduate-level dramaturgy class. I made a clichéd comment lifted from something I'd read in an essay about "commodification," and although uncharacteristic of me, I was, in fact, trying to sound smart. She instantly smelled the crap and snapped, "I don't ever want to hear that term used again." I was bleeding before I knew I was cut. Mine was an inauthentic response. In academe, where everyone wants to sound smart, from the start she pushed me to speak from my truth. I was honored two years later when she offered to be the dramaturg for my graduate thesis production of Soyinke's *The Bacchae of Euripides*. Virginia is a scholar of such high standards that her recognition is a confirmation of your own authority.

From choreographer and dance master Diana Ramos, I learned what it means to be part of a performing arts company. I experienced how rewarding it is to belong to an arts family. Diana was a principal dancer with the Eleo Pomare Dance Company, a seminal choreographer on the leading edge of fierce sociopolitical commentary during the 1960s. Diana danced naked in Central Park to protest the war in Vietnam, a piece of history that greatly impressed us as members of her company, the Diana Ramos Theatre Dance Ensemble. We trusted Diana because she treated us as professionals. Under her tutelage at the University of Massachusetts, I learned how to mount original works in the genre of theater dance. She taught us how to create a textured, seamless collage of movement, music, and language, an approach that became the muscle of my technique as a writer and director.

From Professor Ed Golden, I learned that I was alive and well as an actor. I have never seen anyone coach actors more incisively and with such quick results. After my extended absence from the stage, it was Ed who took my hand and led me past my terror at being under the lights. In graduate school he heard me read a part in a classmate's seminar project and offered a whole heap of academic credits to create the role of Mama in *So Far*. It was an offer I could not refuse. His disarmingly light touch is wholly penetrating; with an almost laid-back air, he pushes actors to dig deeper. He coaxed me to dig deep enough to unearth my dismembered performer and breathe life back into her.

From my directing mentor Professor Dick Trousdell, I learned an invaluable maxim: We have three resources with which to stage a production—human, time, and money—and they are important in that order; your people are your priority, time is of the essence, and the money will come. Dick and I enjoyed engrossing conversations about archetype and process and healing. He spoke in his calm and erudite way, telling me, "Judyie, you're already doing it, part of your coming into a master's program is for you to to see where you are already a master." When Dick was clearing his office in preparation for retirement, he called me in and gestured to his extensive library. "Take whatever you want," he said. There is a particular decorum to the library of a great professor, the shelves filled with books that have been appreciated by generations of students. With reverence I selected my scholarly inheritance.

From my acting mentor Allan Miller, I learned, "We illuminate human behavior." He taught that acting is as much technical as it is inspiration; performance is scientific. "Acting is something here, something not here, and something of yourself," meaning you must be fully present to the moment "here," you must have done your homework "something not here", and you must be connected to the body "something of yourself". His practices of making a sound about how you feel, of extending movement, of extending impulse, of going toward or against an emotion, all remain cornerstones of my teaching. These are ways to stay present, to avoid "acting," to maintain laser focus on "being," so that the performance is spontaneous and fresh, the work is alive, consistent, and, at the same time, unpredictable. Working in his class was the first time I entered "The Zone," the space where you fully inhabit and are completely beyond yourself. Allan let us bright young undergrads at City College's newly established professional school, the Leonard Davis Center for the Performing Arts, know that yes, we had talent and that was only a part of success as an actor. "Frankly, that counts for about forty percent," he told us "the rest is perseverance." Allan gave us acting principles. When you left his instruction, you had tools that would serve you a lifetime.

Standing in my studio, speaking to my students, something will come out of my mouth and I hear the voices of my teachers. My distinguished lineage of artists and scholars is guiding the room.

I'm explaining to my Cape Town students about Theater Time. They are amused.

"Oh Judyie, don't you know about Africa Time?"

"Indeed I do, in the States we have what's called 'CP Time' meaning 'Colored Peoples Time,' and it hinders us just as badly in the States as it does here." In years to come, whenever Brown Paper would perform at festivals or community gatherings, I would always be complimented on our discipline and punctuality. At the Cape Town Festival, a major outdoor event, we covered the performance slot for a big-name professional who was dreadfully late. "I wish all the groups were like your company," the very relieved stage manager said, hugging me. We continued on schedule because "the show must go on."

Anyone who lives for any time in Africa understands the necessary reorientation to time. Much has been written about the concepts of linear/Western time as opposed to circular/Eastern time. Linear time is the drum of the West, one moment after another marching along monotonous and stifling. Linear time is vital in that it keeps us on what could be lifesaving schedules. It also divides us because we become slaves to the clock. We are too busy watching minutes tick by, trying to keep up as our lives shrink, steadily losing what is meaningful. Circular time depends more on feeling and intuition. Actions are taken when the time feels right. Circular time has its own pitfalls when it lacks any sense of urgency, and the need to get something done at a collectively agreed-upon appointment is ignored. Time is a resource and too often squandered waiting for the right moment. I am not advocating linear time over circular time, or vice versa. I am suggesting an evolution into Spiral Time. In Spiral Time, the machine mentality does not control us, nor are we in the choke hold of chance. Spiral Time moves forward with efficiency and stays connected to intuition. We align ourselves with the head and the heart, with feeling and rationality.

"Time is money" is a misconception; time is more than money, because time is the currency of our lives. How do you "spend" your time? Being habitually late is an angry state of mind, it sets up a dynamic of deficit. Being on time speaks to the psyche to affirm that one's artistic life is important. Self-expression is a priority. Being on time is a sign of respect, it establishes the ritual space with precision, it's about showing up for yourself and for your people. It says to the ensemble, "I value your time as well as mine." Ending on time is equally important, it acknowledges that everyone's life goes on and there will be time enough to continue tomorrow.

ᚴ

From the rubble of my crash landing in Cape Town, things are looking up. I have a steady boyfriend, Medi, and my faithful students. Despite this perfectly nice new romance, I'm still clutching to notions of rekindling the ill-fated affair with Mr. Internet Infatuation. He still looks mighty fine. If it's true that a hard head makes a soft behind, then I have the softest rump in the world. Some fantasies die hard. I agree to meet him at a University of Cape Town concert.

I definitely want to look fabulous, which means I won't ride in the *kombi*, the jam-packed overheated collective taxis of Cape Town. I am wearing cream-colored slide heels and want my manicured feet to arrive tidy and cute, makeup intact, and skin cool. Even though it's expensive, I call a private cab that keeps me waiting too long. I finally go downstairs just in time to see the driver pull off with another passenger. "Hey! Yo!" I shout while waving my arms, then leaning in the window to explain that this is my ride and I'm going to be late. A pretty young woman in a flowered dress sits in the front seat holding a suitcase.

"Come on, I'll pay your fare. I've got to get to work, I'm losing money."

"You'll pay the whole ride?" I ask.

"Yes. Get in. Let's go. I'm late." She's starting to panic.

As we wind through the city, she's getting more and more agitated, nagging the driver to run red lights.

"I'll get docked a thousand rand if I'm late."

A thousand rand? Too many people in Cape Town live on less than one thousand rand per month. I get the picture. She works at a gentlemen's club, one of the many sex clubs overflowing during the tourist season's rush of business.

"Just don't turn off the meter," I instruct the driver as we approach her destination.

He mumbles, "Okay," lets the working girl out after she pays him double, and immediately cuts off the meter.

I protest. "Hey, what is this? I told you don't cut the meter."

He silently drives toward the highway.

"Why did you do that?" I'm pissed.

His hostile voice explodes.

"You don't tell me what to do! She's a whore, she sells her body for money."

Now I am angry.

"And what!?" My voice is rising. "You weren't supposed to turn off the meter."

"You Americans," he hisses, "so arrogant, you and your Mr. Bush think you own everyone and everything. Don't think you can tell me what to do."

I flip. Here I am a Black woman managing to live a life of integrity while avoiding the bottom of America's food chain, and I'm supposed to take the heat for some moron presidential poseur. Hell No.

"Don't try it," I snap back. "You can't put that on me."

I notice on his cabbie's license a Muslim name, Amir Jamal. I move closer to the front seat and lean into the mirror. "My name is Al-Bilali. Look at me. My brother looks just like you, we are related." I see his eyes examining my face inches from his. We're on the highway driving at seventy miles per hour, both of us furious. Part of me thinks this is not too smart.

"That tone, you cannot shout at me." His voice is at a dangerous overheated pitch.

"It was not my intention to insult you. I resent being treated unfairly, and besides who are you to judge her? Only Allah can judge."

I can quote the Quran when pressed.

We make eye contact. Abruptly he makes a wrong turn off the expressway.

"Where are you going?" I suspect I'll now get put out on the side of the road.

"A mistake. I turned too early." Unexpectedly he speaks in a civil tone. In that instant, our shouting match softens into a conversation. I sit back quietly while he navigates back to the highway.

"I have a family," he says as the fiery air in the taxi cools off. "This is how I make a living." *Yes,* I thought, *and here's this shake dancer making your annual salary in a month and some American cowboy floozy hiring cars to keep her toenail polish shiny.*

"We are the same, we are closer than we realize." I exhale. I speak gently. "You know you do look like my brother."

"I just didn't like your tone of voice," he concedes.

"It was not my intention to insult." I appreciate this man working hard, exhausted, understanding that he looks like my brother back in the States.

Close to the concert hall he gets lost and we pull over, search his map, and discover together how to get there. I continuously confuse directions as he makes a few more wrong turns. Now we are laughing about driving in circles.

"Just leave me here," I assure him. "I can walk the rest of the way."

"No, sister." He is adamant. "I will take you where you are going."

We do finally arrive. By now I know the number and ages of his children. He knows I am an artist and I teach. I offer him the full fare. He hands it back to me.

"This is enough," he says, holding a few bills.

"Please, for your family," I insist.

We reach a compromise that allows us both to feel generous. At the concert hall Amir Jamal gets out to shake my hand. Impulsively I hug him. I don't know how many lifetimes we have traveled; I do know we have reached the other shore.

ᚾ

I came to Cape Town for a five-week visit. I am here now almost three months. Where before I wanted to run away heartbroken, now I must force myself to get on the plane. Medi has become my grounding cord. He teaches me about the Beautiful Game of soccer, or football, as it is called in most of the world. In the field he is fierce, a commander with all the skill and magnetism of a champion. Out of the field, he is almost inaudible.

"Medi, why can't you be as strong off the pitch as when you are on? Your voice, these people need to hear your voice. That's where your fortune lies."

He doesn't answer. He is mute again. When I ask him about his splendid technique, he shares his philosophy.

"It is simple, Judyie, you just play. It is a game and you must always remember to play."

He teaches me to make tasty stew from canned fish, tomatoes, peppers, onions, and lots of chili, served with a mound of steaming pap. Then he teaches me to make pap, the staple of southern Africa.

He teaches me to rest on Sundays, to relax, to be still.

He teaches me how to bribe cops, not because he's prone to criminal activity, extortion is simply a necessary survival skill to avoid the capricious whims of greedy police. He tells me when they stop you, you let them know you are a footballer, you show them the soccer boots you always carry in your bag along with every other piece of identification: your passport, your refugee status papers, your team ID—every shred of evidence that you exist, that you are not another nameless, faceless, assumed-worthless Black African man.

"You talk nice to them. You tell them what position you play, you talk to them about the game. They love football. You put the money in between the front seats of the car where they can see it. You don't say anything about it. When they pick it up and put it in their pocket, you keep talking nice. Then they leave...They always let me go."

I grow impatient listening to his stories of how he has been hoodwinked time and again, conned into working for no money with only the flimsy promise of a contract. In Cape Town, Johannesburg, Namibia, Congo, in all these places, he allows himself to be used by unscrupulous agents and owners, signed onto a team that will take his time and energy and give back nothing.

"Why do you do it? Why do you keep on trusting these people?" My tone is shrill. I am at wit's end with his naïveté, his being a sucker, being too generous, as though the world cares anything about a big heart.

"I am a professional," he repeats to himself, to me, to anyone who will listen. It's his way of keeping himself sane in the unyielding grip of corruption.

"Then act like one! Speak up! Stop giving it away!" I snap, because in my own sphere of influence, I am guilty of the same thing, of giving it away in my desire for validation.

The men who sleep in the park across from my apartment call out to Medi every morning. "Hey, Rasta! Hey, brother!" They know he plays football. He knows their names and grasps their hands as he says hello. Daily he acknowledges the humanity of people whom most of us ignore. His big heart refuses to be bitter. He teaches me patience.

Finally, I must leave Cape Town. My travel visa is about to expire, and if I stay past the date stamped in my passport, I am subject to deportation. I pack my bags, hug my students good-bye, kiss my devoted darling farewell. Days before I am scheduled to depart, I open the e-mail saying I have received a Fulbright Senior Scholar award. Ingrid is with me at the Internet café when I read the news. We throw our hands up in the air hallelujah-style, holler with joy, and embrace. I will return to South Africa to live and to teach for an entire year.

Journal Entry, New York

I came back to country cold and gray being told it is at war.

Heavy. Like being dipped in lead.

South African poet and activist Diana Ferrus was key to making my Fulbright possible. She brought me to visit the University of the Western Cape and introduced me all around the campus. She arranged for my letter of invitation from UWC's English Department. From the States I send her this grateful postscript:

Dear Diana,

Your keen intuition is correct, it was difficult to leave South Africa and the beautiful people I've become close to—truly it is such a great gift that I'm returning in a matter of months for the Fulbright.

I'm delighted to see my family. They are all doing very well. Still, I had an awful depression that has had me sleepy and lethargic since I arrived. My dear friend and writing partner Valerie describes it as Internal Culture Shock, where the person I've become in the past three months has to integrate herself into life here. I'm not the same woman who landed in Cape Town in January. I like this New Woman very much—I plan to nurture her well.

I understand why I didn't take any snapshots. I couldn't contain the depth of feeling I experienced in small rectangular photos. Even my big pieces of sprawling brown paper only tell part of the story. Any picture I took would need to be in vivid, moving, liquid colors that drip and ooze off the photo surface and have sensation when they touch the skin. That's the intensity of my experience.

Where is Home, I wonder? I have asked this question all my life. My hometown of New York is exhausted and bewildered from the chilly temperatures and the frozen mentality of war. Now is the time to hold Love so firmly in our hearts. I know that my work and my play is to encourage people to listen and heed their wisdom inside, that's what my writing and teaching is about. Being in South Africa gave me that insight.

Much Love,

Your Stateside Sister

It is April when I get back home, a few weeks after the United States has invaded Iraq. On a snowy, early spring day as I soak in a long, hot bath, the words "Brown Paper Studio" appear across my forehead. My newest creative baby has been born.

꙼

Part Two
Making Ground

2004

Gratitude
Motherhood

I dreamed I was an eagle chick on a thousand-foot mountain. It was my birthday and I got an elephant for a present. I was so happy, but my mood changed when my parents wanted to teach me how to fly. I refused and kept eating. A week later my parents flew off to get food and never returned...

The Dream of the Eagle Chick

D'CIPHER: Set the Record Round

Before going to South Africa I had not held any job in my life for more than two years. Along with freelance directing and teaching theater, I've been a cocktail waitress and a clothing boutique clerk on and off because transient work allowed me the freedom to pursue my art. I only occasionally held a well-paid position, which meant our family constantly teetered on a narrow financial ledge. "How do you do it? How do you balance your many lives on apparently thin air?" people asked me. What they want to know is, "What's your hustle?"

If I told them, they wouldn't believe me, because it required we live so uncomfortably close to the edge. You think Harry Potter works magic? Too often our family has stayed afloat through sheer hocus-pocus. By middle-class American standards, we rode at the back of the economic bus, and having to calculate the cost of every single thing every single day took a toll on my children...

Mom...I know you've heard the expression "Ghetto Fabulous"...

The longest place I have ever worked is the University of the Western Cape. My appointment at UWC as a Fulbright scholar was for one year, which I managed to extend into two and stayed on in various roles for five more years. UWC was founded in the 1970s under the apartheid regime as a tertiary institution for Coloured, or mixed-race, South Africans. At that time in not-so-long-ago history, there was no consideration that Black South Africans would go to college. They were viewed as solely the servant class for the white South African supremacist nightmare. UWC has a distinguished history as the "University of the Left" in the struggle against racist oppression. I was enthralled listening to my colleagues recount how they protested, marched, were arrested and sometimes imprisoned, how across lines of colour, class, age, and gender they successfully toppled a malevolent system. I remain awed by their solidarity.

When I landed in Johannesburg in 2002, I was quickly engaged by South Africans of many descriptions who eagerly talked about the social and political progress of their country in the new millennium. This was a welcome contrast to the marked lack of discourse in the States, where we were allowing our Bill of Rights to be eroded under the guise of the Patriot Act. As I listened to South African citizens, I perceived something subtle surfacing in every conversation about what happened in the aftermath of apartheid. There was a slight hesitation in speech, a distinct pause: "since...1994" or "since...democracy" or "since...the new government."

While it is common in the United States, none of the South African citizens I met described the New Dispensation as "postapartheid"; the taste in the mouth was too bitter, the phrase woefully inadequate for the changes in society. There was no uniformly accepted party line. There was no easy answer. My gut response was that this minute silence signified a leap in national identity, and here was an opportunity for artistic research. In that momentarily held inhalation, I imagined vigorous theater-making around self-definition.

By the time I got to Cape Town, the phrase "Memory & Vision" verbalized the ellipsis. I structured my Fulbright proposal to explore its meaning, also naming my graduate-level course at the UWC's English Department "Memory & Vision: Theater Practice and Social Issues." In designing the curriculum, I selected four plays that were all created from conducting interviews: *The Laramie Project, Polaroid Stories, The Vagina Monologues,* and *Twilight: Los Angeles 1992.* Each is very different in style and production development. The first half of the course is conducted as a seminar, with small groups of students assigned to each play. They research information on the playwright and the play's production history and dramaturgy, prepare questions for discussion, and present an excerpt of the script. In the second half of the semester, each student identifies a political or social issue of interest—preferably related to southern Africa—conducts interviews, and writes a short play. The plays go through a first-draft reading, rewrites, and onto a final showing celebration, complete with invited audience and refreshments.

It's the first day of Memory & Vision at UWC. I greet my group of fifteen graduate students with a typically informal American howdy-do:

"Hi, I'm Judyie Al-Bilali, please call me Judyie…"

I introduce myself as an artist who teaches and launch straight into a couple of humongous philosophical questions:

"What is the role of theater in our highly technological twenty-first century? What is unique and necessary about live performance in our global society?"

Polite silence.

Okay granted, it's more than a mouthful, perhaps the topics are too chewy. I coax from a different angle:

"Tell me something about your personal experiences with art as a catalyst for social change. How can creativity be used as a force for transformation?"

Blank stares.

Yikes! I'm dying up here. Not a hint of response.

I want to unlock these attentive, reserved students. In subsequent sessions, I discover this seminar format is new to most of my class. Right now I sense their scrumptious ideas are simmering very close to the surface. I gamble that an impromptu writing session will get us unstuck:

"Imagine you have just been elected president of the New South Africa. Take out your notebooks and write for fifteen minutes, addressing your country on inauguration day. No editing, no crossing out, I don't care about spelling, grammar, or punctuation—I just want to hear your voice."

Nervous fidgeting.

I hit the accelerator, driving fast:

"Tell your people, who have just placed absolute confidence in you, about the vast possibilities of this newest of nations. Dream big! If you don't know what to say, then just write over and over, 'I don't know what to write.' until your body says, 'This is what I know,' and trust the words that come out. Don't think too much. Welcome contradictions. We are stepping into the world of theater, and contradictions are about being human. Don't worry about it making sense, because no one comes to the theater for rationality. Put your heads down and go. I'll tell you when fifteen minutes is up."

Don't think too much!

Is this woman kidding?

They push past their resistance. They write. They read their writing out loud. Their writing is strong. They are hooked on their own voice.

"Congratulations, you have just written your first monologues."

As we conclude, a student claps his hands, nodding his head vigorously. "I've been waiting three years for this class."

In the weeks that follow, our conversations become so engaged we invariably run out of time, with all of us scrambling to make the last trains and taxis home in the evening. That cramped third-floor classroom is the first blush of Brown Paper Studio, several students will accompany me and Salim across campus to become founding members.

The students' plays in Memory & Vision are about religious repression, homosexuality, Hip Hop culture, domestic violence, modern-day fairy tales, expatriate homesickness, political corruption, and more. As I listen to the first eager, clumsy drafts, I resolve to mount these new works as staged readings for a wider university audience. By democratic process, the class chooses four plays to be presented as "New Plays by Postgrads." Students who had little or no experience in theater are identifying themselves as writers, directors, actors, designers, and dramaturgs.

In the class are two men from Rwanda. One is round and jovial, with a prominent scar across his chin where he was gashed by a machete during the 1994 holocaust. For over a year, he has been away from his wife and infant daughter still in Kigali. Like many displaced African people, he manages to maintain an air of optimism despite his extended separation. The other student from Rwanda is thin and quiet, his language and social skills poor. For their play assignment, the men choose to write about Rwanda's civil war culminated by the genocide perpetrated against the Tutsis.

At the beginning of the semester, before the play submissions are due, I evaluate my students' writing proficiencies with a short assignment. My awkward, taciturn student hands in an obviously plagiarized paper. After uttering fewer than two sentences in the entire class, he submits a very sophisticated essay about South African theater after the democratic elections. I am in a dilemma. It is my first semester teaching in a foreign country, and I'm faced with what is a difficult situation for any instructor. I defer to my department chair, a deeply caring professor who tutors the student into producing, albeit badly written, an original essay. I appreciate my chair's compassion. Neither of us wants this young man to fail.

When the student in question presents his script at our final readings, it is poignantly clear how theater allows us to express our deepest selves. His play begins very much like feuding Montagues and Capulets except that we hear Hutus and Tutsis in a raging argument in the village center. This writing is most certainly original. It is his voice we have not heard all semester surfacing though a horrific story. The final moments of the script again take place in the village center. We sit riveted as several characters confess their war crimes in haunting litanies:

"My name is Kamana of the family of Muzindutsi, I am a Hutu from the tribe of Abazigaba and I am guilty of committing these crimes: the rape of Nzamukosha, the young daughter of Mutunzi that I killed a few hours before; the murder of Kalimunda's entire family, I played a big role in the mutilation of Mushumba and his wife who were our immediate neighbors. For all these innocent persons I killed and mutilated, I ask forgiveness to the survivors of their families; to the Tutsi group members who used to live on this hill; to all Rwandese and to the country as a whole."

Over and over, as the fictionalized names change, the actors describe atrocities, express guilt, make pleas for forgiveness. The intensity gives us just a glimpse of what this introverted, almost invisible man has experienced. What he has endured is almost too difficult for us to hear.

His compatriot writes a compelling play with a long academic title more suitable for an essay than a drama. In the talkback after his reading, I question one of the most provocative lines.

"In your script you quote a statistic 'one million people dying violently in a hundred days.' Is that accurate?"

"That was the death toll in my country."

"Then that is your title, *One Million People in One Hundred Days.*"

In teaching Memory & Vision, I practice applying creativity to constructing a new society. I recognize how making theater can support

the process of transformation. I realize that people can write insight-
ful, expressive plays if you don't tell them that playwriting is difficult.
I'm eager to share what I know about Art and Theater and Life in this
foreign and familiar country. I am grateful that my students are my
teachers.

Gratitude...

*Because it sounds nicely spiritual, I thought Gratitude ought to be the number
one Brown Paper Studio basic. Since I'm a pragmatic director and arriving on time
is such an issue for us members of the African Diaspora, I decide "Be On Time" is
at the top of the list. It has to do with making oneself a priority. Making one's creative
life most important is very spiritual. Nothing can begin until we are all gathered, and
your presence is valuable. Once that happens, we can express our collective apprecia-
tion. I open the space with a silent moment for company members to express "thanks
for the opportunity to create something of beauty and excellence together." That's one of
the first phrases you hear in Brown Paper, to offer thanks to whoever or whatever or
wherever you consider your spiritual source. It can be the Ancestors, the Great Spirit,
the Universe, God, or Your Very Own Being. It says, "Yes, I made it, I showed up
for myself."*

It's a hike to the other side of campus, and I'm doing my best to
keep up with notoriously fast-paced Miki, my most welcoming of
colleagues in the English Department. I have just arrived at UWC,
and she wants to introduce me to the director of the Centre for the
Performing Arts to secure space for a theater studio. Miki has taught

English to two generations of Black and Coloured students in Cape Town. She is well-known by many families because her father taught some of her students' parents. She was raised by German immigrant parents on a wine farm in the lush Stellenbosch valley; they lived in the Coloured area, stubbornly resisting relocation under apartheid rule. Miki grew up immersed in Black and Coloured South African culture. My new friend is a humanitarian, a soft-spoken and relentless freedom fighter. Wherever we go, in any community, she commands the utmost respect.

On this day at the end of February, the weather is exquisite, a warm and golden late summer afternoon in the Western Cape. Miki wants me to offer students something that does not exist at UWC: an extracurricular theater class, a space to study performing arts, a chance to be on stage. I'm trotting to keep stride with this woman who will become my guardian angel in South Africa. When I'm discouraged, homesick, lovesick, broke, or all of the above, she'll feed me and we'll drink wine and focus on what's most important to us both: the expression of beauty in the world. Sometimes when we are together, I endearingly call her by her full name, Marika Magarethe, because it is so musical.

Miki introduces me to the senior professor who is the director of the Centre for the Performing Arts. He is an elder academic who favors classical music. As a Fulbright scholar, he spent time at a university in the southern United States, and he approves of me because we are both of the Fulbright pedigree. He magnanimously opens the door to an enormous room with high ceilings and huge windows. The space is flooded with light, and outside there are trees. This kind of space and access is unheard-of in the States. I'm blown away by my good fortune.

I schedule Brown Paper Studio every Wednesday and Thursday from one to three p.m. After loud, hilarious rehearsals, where we blast Hip Hop, jazz, and R&B, students hang around on the steps outside, chatting and smoking cigarettes and looking strange. Theater always attracts the lunatic fringe, and we lunatics take over. Participants are painted and pierced with unruly hair and tattoos. Most significantly, they are every color and description of South African and foreign student. The legacy of apartheid haunts the campus in the persistent and insidious divisions between Black and Coloured students. What makes Brown Paper Studio visible and ultimately successful at UWC is that our group crosses the racial boundaries. Students are given the possibility of a totally new identity, that of being an artist. It is a joy to see brown, black, and white people walking arm in arm across campus, laughing in the cafeteria, riding transport together. We become a hub of creativity, a place where the rigid lines dividing youth on campus dissolve.

Word spreads fast. More than sixty students walk through the doors to sign up for Brown Paper Studio. Of that number, twenty-eight will stay the course, remaining to rehearse on Wednesdays, Thursdays, weekends, and holidays to produce our first original performance, *D'CIPHER: Set the Record Round*. We use the method of devised theater, a fairly recent term for the long-standing process in which work is created collaboratively by a group of people, rather than a single writer. It is my practice to assign actors the words of other writers to perform. It can be astonishing to hear one's language spoken by another company member, very often revealing a new meanings and depth. I always incorporate at least one piece of writing from everyone in the ensemble. Dramaturgically, this confirms the concept of gestalt, that the whole is greater than the sum of its parts. As we put the work on its feet, I can see that, stereotypes aside, my South African company members have grown up in communities that sing. These young actors intrinsically understand harmony, layering, repetition, call and response—all musical elements that characterize my directing style. Without any formal stage training, they have an affinity for language and improvisation that moves the development of our script along at a rapid pace. They request that we rehearse over the Easter break. I'm amazed that students are willing to forfeit their vacation and am honestly doubtful they will really show up. On Sunday night I buy plenty of food for sandwiches and baskets of fruit, and it's a good thing I do, because everybody is there every day.

In all the years in South Africa, I never conduct auditions for any show. There is so much talent in such need of creative outlet that as long as an actor can commit to the rehearsal schedule and respect the basics of the studio, I put them on stage. Even when I state this policy at the outset, students do not believe me. Their jaws drop in amazement when I read the cast list and put a script in their hands on the first day of rehearsal. In the impromptu space of Brown Paper Studio, many company members discover an unfettered sense of self. For some it is new terrain free of the strict codes of familial and social conformity. They are relieved to no longer be outcasts, covertly or overtly "different." They are part of the Universal Tribe of Theater. Here they are welcomed as renegades.

On campus Brown Paper Studio is a catalyst for change, for a growing sense of unity in student life. Our company stands out, and it is the reason we receive support from the university's administration. They are wise enough to encourage an initiative that builds bridges. The

Centre for the Performing Arts' director will eventually have regrets when he realizes that a theater company is rambunctious and messy and difficult to dislodge. I'm sure he wanted the building to project a stately, music-conservatory atmosphere. Alas, while I am in residence, it is not meant to be.

"Mommy, here I am, this is when I'm looking for you." My three-year-old son, Salim, displays his abstract rendering done in crayon. It's a young child's multicolored drawing full of excited lines and squiggles and circles. Salim's cherub face, with those seductively long eyelashes seemingly bestowed only on boys, lights up. He snuggles closer to me, points to one of the shapes, and intently continues his narrative. "See, I'm flying around in the sky. I'm looking for you and they want to help me and I tell them I know where you are and when I find you I am so happy." He has illustrated the story of his arrival from the spirit world into my womb. He remembers that he and I have an agreement to meet in this life as mother and son, and the "they" he refers to are the angels that offered to guide him. As a newly incarnating soul, he was confident he would find his destination—me. I'm grateful his otherworldly memories are still intact and wonder how long before the rigid left-brained educational system discounts his visions as "only make-believe." "That's beautiful son, you really remember all that?" He nods yes, turns to me, and with his baby-boy smile adds, "I was very glad to meet Daddy, too."

Salim is now seventeen. I have told him this story many times as he is growing up to remind him of our sacred contract. He is accompanying me in South Africa for the first half of my academic year as a Fulbright scholar. At dinner after the first Memory & Vision class, I wonder out loud to him why the grad students were so reticent. "It's okay, Mom," he assures me. "They just don't know you yet. Young people don't want to open textbooks, they want to open their hearts and minds. They'll see."

Mom. . .I know you've heard the expression Ghetto Fabulous. . .Well, that's not really us because we don't live in the ghetto. . .

My son, who has grown up on the roller-coaster of fulfillment and disappointment that is the life of an artist, is by my side at the genesis of Brown Paper Studio. It could not have happened without him. His easy presence helps define these first days and weeks and months. Every Wednesday and Thursday afternoon, we haul the boom box and brown paper and colored markers and bags of fruit across campus to the Centre for the Performing Arts. Salim knows my process so well; he was hearing these words since before birth. He is a model for participation in the studio. He is punctual, attentive, engaged. He allows himself to be vulnerable and committed. He is gentle, he is funny, he takes artistic risks. As resident DJ, he keeps a common language of beats and rhymes flowing while we invent ourselves and our process. He knows what I do, he believes in what I do, and even when I have flickers of doubt, he holds me steady. When cast members who have never been onstage start to fear if our original play will be ready, the inevitable panic erupts two weeks out from the show's opening. Salim states calmly and unequivocally to the entire company, "If my mom says we'll be ready, we'll be ready." And we are. Salim and I have been together on this road since the beginning. He is my great comfort in this uncharted territory.

Perhaps you have some idea of how many people secretly want to be actors, a hidden desire reflected in our adoration of stage and screen stars. In Brown Paper they can finally admit, "I always wanted to act." Performance is a natural impulse; children dress up and make believe as they try on different versions of themselves. The Studio is a chance to play at being various people in a safe atmosphere. Too soon in our development as human beings, we are told to pick one aspect of our self, an identity that society sanctions and can control, and stick to it. Step too far away from the approved persona and you risk being called crazy or difficult or unstable or an artist. Quite the contrary, it's healthy to act up and out, because suppressing our multiple personalities invites madness and pathology. The Studio encourages taking off the acceptable mask to reveal a whole, multifaceted person.

Who am I? What do I want? How do I get it?

A simple mantra I've adapted for my students, the synthesis of over thirty years of acting training and practice.

Who am I?

Begin with the character's name, age, physical description. I require a thorough written character analysis that includes all the information gathered from the script, along with what the actor's imagination suggests—all the details of the moment, the scene, the temperature, light, time of day, smells, and sounds. It's about creating the realest imaginary world possible. "Who am I?" has to be understood in relation to every other character in the script.

What do I want?

The answer is known as objective, or in more old-school terms, as motivation. It is the desire that drives the scene. Desire is the fuel of creation. If you don't know why you're onstage, we as audience won't know either. And we won't care.

How do I get it?

Use every tactic possible. Actively, physically, in real time, get what you want. I teach the technique of "going toward or against." "Going toward" is to be completely honest about what's happening with you, the actor, and expressing it through the text. "Going against" is to lie like crazy, to cover it up and make us believe the lie. One will necessarily switch in any scene, making split-second choices to go toward or against, just the way we do in life. How often do we lie about our feelings? How often do we expose our truth? It requires being in touch with the body, and the only way to do that is through the ultimate lifeline, the breath. As a director, I have to be able to turn the sound off in the scene and know clearly what's happening. The story is on the body. Body is text.

I adore coaching actors because I have fine-tuned my sensors to read the frequencies coming off the body. I learned early how to trust physical impulses onstage—they lead us to the subterranean complexity, pathos, and radiance of human behavior. We illuminate human behavior so we can live better on this earth. That's how big acting is to me. That's why I treat all actors with the utmost respect. They offer themselves as willing and able channels for all aspects of what it means to Be Human, from the most noble to the most monstrous. They face the disturbing, liberating truth that every character they play is somewhere inside them, and once that emotional reality is excavated, they are different. Their range is from the heavens to the underworld and back again.

Gratitude...

We also express gratitude when the work stinks. When it's raw, rough, boring, when people are showing their asses and acting the fool, because I promise you they will. All of this creative cow dung is fertilizer, what we use to grow human gardens. There is no creativity without shadow, without the devil, without the part you don't want to deal with. What makes the photograph luminous is its quality of light and dark. The key to the chiaroscuro snapshot of your life is the ability to embrace both.

When I was in third grade, my parents bought Miriam Makeba's debut album released in the United States. On the cover photo, Ms. Makeba was dressed in an elegant blue silk gown. Her hair was a short natural, the first I'd seen. She had a charming smile, her arms reached gracefully upward. As I stared at the picture, I must have played "The Click Song" hundreds of times, imitating the words and rhythmic clicks. I was enchanted to the core of my DNA. Sometimes while sitting smashed together with the rest of the city's population in Cape Town taxis, I close my eyes and listen to the languages around: subtle, tonal, forceful, languid. People switch codes in a heartbeat, able to choose which tongue to speak depending on who they're talking to and what they're talking about. Xhosa has a variety of click sounds, and slowly I learn to distinguish where in the mouth they fall, either on the side, center, or top-front palate. At home in private, I'm a child holding an album cover all over again, gleefully practicing these intricate sounds.

My use of English becomes more precise living in a country where language is rich and nourishing. Grade-school children have more fluent, refined English than many American college students. African people are incredulous when we say we speak only one language; they think we must have misunderstood the question "What languages do you speak?" and we stutter, "like, uh...'ya know...English?" It's as though an entire nation chose to ignore its left hand or to hop around on one foot. Being multilingual expands the brain. To look at an object and have several representative sounds for it enhances the intellect.

Exploring language proves to be key in Brown Paper Studio's evolution. I quickly smell the postcolonial dominance around the use of English. The language is both resented and admired. I ask my students, both Afrikaans- and Xhosa-speaking, to teach me phrases, because then I am the one who doesn't know. They are the experts. I am the learner.

Tensions arise when the first draft of *D'CIPHER: Set the Record Round* contains Afrikaans and English, no Xhosa. After we read it through, the company's Xhosa speakers spontaneously launch into a long riff in their mother tongue. They share uproarious jokes, nod at private insights. The rehearsal comes to a standstill as all others sit ignorant of what is being said. I don't interrupt. I don't ask for translation. They let us know in no uncertain terms that the script is incomplete. I ask the Xhosa speakers to teach us the clicks so we can properly pronounce text in performance. Cast members who speak English and Afrikaans stand in a circle humbly experimenting with what our tutors have known since childhood.

While groping our way across the land mines of so-called race, one student just explodes:

"I can't stand it! I'm so sick of this Black/Coloured thing!"

We all are. We use multilingualism to grow. From now on we will be known by our "Mother Tongues," which becomes the title of our final scene in *D'CIPHER*, where we perform an excerpt of Mandela's famous 1994 inauguration speech. The call is in English, and the response comes from all the mother tongues of our international company: twelve official languages of South Africa, including sign language, plus the languages of Uganda, Russia, Kenya, and Sweden. You are free to respond in any language you choose.

During any show, I'm most comfortable backstage or in the lobby. My company wonders why I don't sit in the audience. At first they feel slighted, wanting me to watch and see how good they are. Still compulsively directing in my head, I feel trapped in a seat. I fidget and want to change things, mumble to myself, uselessly wave my hands making adjustments. I can best let go while just listening to the actors and to the audience. I actually calm myself surrounded by the crazy energy of entrances and exits, the fireworks eyes and wired-up drive, as performers move on and offstage. I hear the show in order to give notes for the next one. I sit in the audience once the baby is fully down the birth canal. Emotionally I've cut the umbilical cord, so the work can breathe on its own.

. . .I was alone and ate the rotting elephant carcass. Everyone else's families around were so happy, and my peers were flying past with houses, cars, and girlfriends. Later on I noticed everyone was gone and the mountain started shaking...

The Dream of the Eagle Chick

I was drowning. I was suffocating and losing air, and this could not possibly be my life. Working at a government arts agency was my first and only "good job" with a decent salary and benefits. Fortunately I had health insurance, because the good job almost killed me. Being a bureaucrat, shuffling papers, writing monotonous reports, showing up at a certain time every day and leaving at a certain time every day at an office where I didn't want to be in the first place was choking me. I was actually relieved when, due to budget cutbacks, I was fired in July 1991. My pink slip came too late. Cancer had grown a grapefruit-sized tumor that crushed my lung and developed into pneumonia. My chest was filled with water. I guess I did drown.

I was in a strained marriage and having a hard time being a wife and a mother and a daughter and an employee and an artist. Working as a civil servant, my creative self was neglected; she figured, "If I can't live, none of you can." I wrote a series of poems and short pieces titled *Breathing for Myself*, because I was breathing for too many people. My manuscript got shoved into a desk drawer. Remembering the last days of our family before the divorce, I have an image of a huge ice glacier cracking and crashing into the sea under the heat of my desire for freedom. Only now, when my children are grown, can I bear to hear the truth about me as a mother. My daughter accuses me, "You were never really present." My son echoes the sentiment. If I wasn't present, where was I? I was moving myself and my family around from place to place, possessed by my own internal compass for change, positive I was moving the whole world toward its future.

The children of artists endure a special torture; they must share their parents with Art, inanimate offspring that too often overshadow the flesh-and-blood counterparts. These voracious creations are unpredictable; they invade at any time and consume Mother's precious attention. An artist's daughter or son watches helplessly as Mommy exists in that simultaneously focused and distracted place of gestating a new piece of writing or theater or choreography. She is oddly distant, it appears that nothing is more important—"even me," fears the abandoned child. The children of artists are proud and resentful of their parents' achievements. I cooked meals, I participated in school activities, I loved their father and their grandparents, I maintained a pleasant home, while part of me was often elsewhere. Did I know I was a half-assed mom? Not until I was dreadfully sick, too ill to move. Confined to lying on the living-room couch, I finally watched the videos of my children's Christmas pageants. I had only attended the very last of their kindergarten performances. As I lay in pain, I thought, *Where have I been all these years while they were dressing up as angels and singing sweet carols?* I was at a job, overworked, convinced that someone or something else needed me. How could my children possibly have known my love for them is the fuel that keeps the stars burning?

Mom. . .

I know you've heard the expression Ghetto Fabulous. Well, that's not really us because we don't live in the ghetto. It's like we're supposed to be middle class but without the money, and is that what it means to be working class, and what class are you in if you have artist parents? We're Fabulously Ghetto. . .

We're Fabulously Ghetto because we live on the Upper West Side and went to Dalton when we were little with some of the richest kids in America. You know what it's like to be one of the poorest kids in a rich school? It's confusing. You're not poor at all.

When you're a kid and you go to birthday parties and it's a big chore because your mom gets pissed off at having to buy gifts for rich kids who "don't need a damn thing," but you can't come empty-handed to birthday party catered at an expensive East Side restaurant with magicians and clowns hired for entertainment...so why can't you just keep the rich kids' gifts that they don't need?

One day you realize shopping for clothes is more about the price tag than the clothes, and it's never really fun again because it stresses your mother out and she's not supposed to get stressed out because she had cancer and almost died. And speaking of clothes, your grandma started the first super-fancy high-fashion business owned by Black people in New York, and it's still hard to make the rent every month.

We're Fabulously Ghetto when we live year-round in our summer house in Edgartown on Martha's Vineyard, the world-famous resort community that attracts a lot of shi-shi Black folks and where Dad is a school janitor and Mom is a clerk in a dress shop earning minimum wage when she's not a theater professional out directing plays in different parts of the country and Dad comes home at night and creates sculptures that sell for thousands of dollars. We have to eat buckets of homemade chicken soup with saltine crackers because it's cheap.

When you're Muslim in a Christian world and you're Black in a White world and the only pictures in your house are people like Mandela and Malcolm and family photos from a Black settlement founded by your ancestors in Kentucky and artwork from Africa.

When you're in third grade in rural New England and your parents drop you off at school in the woods and they're blasting Rick James' "Superfreak" at seven forty-five a.m. and you're embarrassed cause you're weird enough already...

So what are you anyway?

You're Fabulously Ghetto.

To understand my children, you must know their father. Shahid is a man who has his own mind. When he offers his analysis of a political or social situation, *everybody* in the room stops to listen. His wisdom comes from the streets and from being a self-educated scholar. Long before anyone was talking about "going green,'" Shahid was an environmentalist. In poor Black communities, he recycled enough materials to build houses and theaters and communal spaces. He is a philosopher and a political scientist. He is an artist and activist. He was a Black Panther, a Black Muslim, a Black Everything. He is at once a Nationalist and a Universalist and understands that these definitions are not mutually exclusive. To survive as Black people, we are required to have multiple identities.

Shahid is a devoted father. He taught our children to honor their relationship as brother and sister. I didn't know anything about that kind of rapport. I was raised without any understanding of a bond between siblings. Every night before Hanan went to sleep, her father would come in to say goodnight and turn the lighted globe by the side of the bed so that Africa was facing her. Every night he methodically set her eyes on the Motherland.

Shahid supported my art, my work, and my vision one hundred percent. So how could I initiate a divorce? How could I have the audacity to break up a family? Even as I gained strength and confidence in my profession, our marriage caused me to disintegrate emotionally. I was never sure that I was loved just for being me, just for being a woman. To be valued, I felt pressured to prove I was productive. I had recurring dreams of flirting with some other man, or even about to become intimate with an old lover when I suddenly remember I was married.

I'd be surprised and tickled and embarrassed, and I would stop my promiscuous behavior. Although in my dreams I was faithful, in my waking life, I was unfulfilled. I was buried under responsibility. My husband and I were in a vise of lost communication. We were dragging along on obligation and routine. The restless tectonic plates of my soul knew I needed more.

At the end of 2003, I visited Cape Town, ostensibly for a writing sabbatical. With a fat fellowship in hand, I had time, money, and a brand-new computer. Really and truly I wanted to sleep in my dear Medi's arms. Once again I hopped on a plane for the charms of a younger man; fortunately this time, this one adores me. I am incorrigible.

Now in 2004 our unlikely union must expand to include Salim, when he and I arrive for my first year as a Fulbright scholar. It's a bit touchier than Stella and Her Groove, because at seventeen my son is potentially sexually active and the man his mom is sleeping with is of ambiguous age. Boy and Boyfriend play video games together, then at some point, it's lights out and everyone goes to bed. By trial and error, Salim and Medi forge an awkward alliance that allows us to be an unusual household far away from our respective homes.

Medi takes Salim under his very caring wing, introducing him to life in Africa in a way that makes my son more than a visitor. Did he resent his mother's young lover? I'm sure he did. He could also see that I was happy, and right in the midst of his being at least resigned to the situation, he falls in love with a pretty and emotionally complex

South African college student. "The apple doth not fall far from the tree" and like his mother, my son falls hard. For the next few years, pursuit of his beloved shapes his world on both sides of the ocean. We are all drawn to South Africa, Salim and I because we feel more at home living overseas than in our own country, Medi because his homeland is hell.

Medi was not always a refugee, a term he came to loathe as his years in exile piled up. He was raised in a solid middle-class family in the capital city of Kinshasa. His family lived on their own land, with a spacious house, a backyard, fruit trees, and pets. There were cars in the driveway, his parents' Volkswagen parked next to his uncle's Mercedes-Benz. His grandfather was the owner of a carpentry factory with many employees manufacturing doors, chairs, and desks for the school system. Adults in Medi's household went to work at white-collar jobs. They traveled on vacations. Inside his home were nice clothes, record players, dining rooms with china dishes and glassware. He was not raised trudging from place to place, carrying only a couple of suitcases, his soccer trophies, and photo albums of a real life he left behind. As a "displaced person," he would gradually accumulate a few belongings, a mattress, a TV, a small fridge, only to have to sell them again when work became scarce, and then start anew.

Before he left Congo, Medi was studying to be a lawyer at university. As civil unrest escalated into civil war, the military marched daily onto campus, disrupting classes and harassing young men to enlist. Being a soldier was not an option—this man eats only fish and vegetables and would rather escort insects out of the house than kill them. He left DRC, traveling first to Tanzania, spending time in Madagascar, and finally landing in South Africa, where his superior soccer skill immediately earned him a contract with a first-division team in Cape Town. What he was sure meant a change in destiny turned out to be another false start. The club owner was an infamous crook, and the whole business went belly-up, owing Medi over $2,000, the equivalent of several months' salary. It was at this moment our lives intersected. Unable to recover his wages, he was evicted from his apartment and resumed the cycle of selling his belongings to eat. I watched him keep gaining and losing ground, always with the status of refugee on his head. Through him I came to understand that many of the foreign nationals I saw sitting for long hot days in the marketplace selling boring paintings and bangle bracelets to tourists, or standing for long cold nights wearing bright orange vests serving as car guards for small tips and smaller wages, had been professionals in their own countries: doctors, teachers, nurses, architects, accountants. Their plight put his constant "I am a professional" in context.

An affair with a younger man is a tightrope. You will fall off, you will get bruised. One afternoon while Ingrid and I wait at the bus stop, a woman notices I'm wearing Medi's soccer jacket. "Oh! Does your son play for that team?" she exclaims. Ingrid bursts out laughing. I'm mortified. When Medi is injured playing, she slyly recommends, "Take him over to pediatrics." Like a hired driver, he drops me off at chic cocktail parties and formal embassy dinners, comes back later, and waits in the car. Our difference in age not only has its stupid moments, at times it nearly destroys us.

Still, we are lovers—in love with each other, with ourselves, with Cape Town.

Cape Town is a woman. She is willful, gorgeous, moody, passionate. Her weather is a temper tantrum, a petulant rainy morning, a flamboyant sunny afternoon, a lusty starry night. Table Mountain curves in a massive stone embrace, hugging the city tight against its bosom, defying the tug of the ocean. When it is hot, you can feel the pavement burning up through your shoes, when it is cold, the rain becomes ice driving sideways so hard umbrellas are useless. Summer wind shrieks like a demon. You never tire of the vast, primal sky and shape-shifting clouds. The light will make you swear you are dreaming.

Cape Town is a dramatic woman, a jealous mistress, a temptress, and a mother. Her official name is the Mother City, and she does nourish you with outrageous food: fresh fish grilled perfectly with lemon and herbs, succulent and savory lamb slow-cooked in rich red wine till it falls off the bone, or curried and wrapped in buttery rotis pungent with chili and chutney. Vegetables in every color piled high on corner stands promise creamy avocado sandwiches, spicy butternut soup, salads of sweet tomatoes and cucumbers and carrots, side dishes of mushrooms and squash and cabbage and green beans. Mangoes and pineapples smell like sugar. Everything gets washed down with world-class chardonnay or cabernet sauvignon or chenin blanc or pinotage or sparkling white wine. Bottles of the best, old vintages and new, shared at sundown or deep into the night, poured with hearty cheers and heartfelt philosophy.

Cape Town is an African woman. She will seduce you.

The city's most famous nightlife strip is Long Street, effervescent with nightclubs, lounges, shops, and restaurants. Medi and I live close to a well-known hangout, a poolroom, dance club, and bar that is his favorite nighttime haunt.

"You know the Pakistani guy?" my sweetie asks me one morning. I don't want to be too conversational. He came in many hours late and despite my rather prickly attitude, coaxed me out of some pussy.

"Yeah, what about him?"

"I play him last night, him and his friend, me and Lito play and win."

"Yeah, so?"

"So he say to me after we win one game, you're lucky - lucky game. It's no luck, I tell him, 'I win you,' then he laughs and says to me again 'lucky.'"

I can see the guy's face, he's older, close to my age, in a bar full of twentysomethings. He's a cool, confident player. I can see his disdainful expression.

"I tell him 'I win you,'" reports my Honey Bun. "I win you. If I no win, I no play again."

"You said that?"

"Yeah, then the guy he say to me, 'You mean if I beat you the next game, you won't play me again?'"

My Pooh Bear's eyes are getting bright recalling last night's contest.

"No, I say to him. If I no win you, I no play here again, not on this table, not in this club. If I am here, I watch. Only watch."

I am lying in bed staring at the ceiling. I don't want to be bothered with this tale. I am busy having an attitude. Now I turn to look at him, his beautiful dreadlocked hair and seal-brown skin and compact body. Now my eyes are bright.

"You said that?" I repeat myself.

I can just imagine the scene in this packed saloon. The techno-funk music blasting, the noisy crowded booths leading to the back room where

the wagers in coins are stacked neatly on the side of the pool table and
the all-night players attract the weed smokers and the weed sellers, the
hustlers and curious and locals and tourists. It's a Wild West drama,
and when my soft-spoken baby throws down this challenge, everyone
draws a quick breath. This is his hangout. His turf. He is known and
greeted warmly when he walks in the door. He doesn't pay for much
because all the soccer fans, refugees and South Africans alike, admire
this sharp, strong footballer from Congo. Royalty in exile. "Le Grand
Jouer," his title in the streets of Cape Town.

"If you win, I no play again." This is a duel. "I win you."

Everyone backs up while the weapons, the pool cues, are drawn. The
white girls throw up their petticoats, and the tiny Coloured woman,
who sits every night cross-legged on the edge of the barstool like she was
born there, smiles slowly, lights her perpetual cigarette, and sucks on a
Heineken half the size of her body. The black busboy in an apron and
baseball cap comes out of the kitchen, pretends to gather empty glasses,
settles in to witness the showdown. The partners step to the table, and
all others press against the wall. All bets are off until this game is played.

I turn my body fully toward him now. It must have a happy ending,
otherwise he would not be telling me. I settle in for the story. If I were
wearing panties, they'd be damp.

"We are playing good, but you know he is good and the shots go in,
go in." He often repeats himself in the most adorable way. "We lose
shots, one of their shots go in, my friend Lito says, he says to me 'we
are going to lose.' I say to him, 'Don't ever say that.'"

I wonder in what language he cautioned Lito. French? Lingala?
Swahili? Certainly not English, the common language of the room.
Quietly he asserts, "We will win."

My Dear One goes on to explain in luscious detail each shot as the game builds to a climax. I don't understand any of it except that I'm really wet now. I'd already forgiven him his transgressions of last night, his promise to be home in a little while, telling me he'll be home 'round midnight, then ringing the bell, red-eyed and reeking of smoke, at four a.m. Now he's managed to make his partying heroic.

"Then at the end I take the shot, I hit the eight ball, the black ball, into the pocket. At the last moment, we win. He knows I am good. It is not luck. I am good."

The eight ball in the pocket, the neocolonial politics of pool. The white ball controls the table, dominates all the colors on the green felt of the planet, yet it is the black ball that decides the game.

I reach for him. He has won me.

On the phone long distance, I tell my girlfriend this story. She sucks her teeth.

"Nigga probably lying."

"So what? You know I still gave him some."

All she and I can do is laugh.

Gratitude. . .

   sets an uplifting tone that gets us all on the same page of celebrating Being Human. The artistic process exposes us. We fall down, bump our egos, knock up against each other, run away from and ultimately embrace the shadow. It's not all pretty and not at all politically correct. It is the unauthorized version of living. We are different at the beginning of a performance project than at the end. We have to change, and that's why we have creative spaces. Staying the same means we are afraid to risk, and often that's where the magic is—it's certainly part of the fun. One of the great rewards of theater is watching us all march, crawl, and leap from that first moment of expressing Gratitude in the Circle to the final moment taking our bows onstage.

While recuperating from cancer, I lived year-round with my husband and children on Martha's Vineyard. I spent one of those slow, restorative years making theater with a group of midlife women. We called ourselves the Black Kettle Sisters. We met every Monday to play games, improvise, and create original performance pieces. As with most theater families, ours was transient. By the end of that year, our eldest member died of cancer, and our youngest member, who had been pronounced infertile by the medical establishment, miraculously conceived and birthed a baby girl.

A cornerstone of Brown Paper Studio practice is a technique I gathered during that year, what I call Dreamscapes. Dreams are ideal material for improvisation because the imagery is wild, vivid, sensual, mercurial. Company members record their dreams in their journals, and the only restriction for dreams used in the studio is that they can't be too erotic or too traumatic. The cast is five actors: the dreamer and four dreamees. The dreamer stands on a chair to read their written dream, choosing one person to play them as the central character and who wears a scarf around their neck to designate them as "I." Actors embody all the elements, including quality of light, emotion, colors, objects, sound, sensation, people, animals—everything. The actors must relate to each other as the dream plot progresses—making strong choices quickly. If there's nothing to do in the dream at the moment, they must simply hold the energy and remain motionless in a well-defined position until another impulse animates them. It is an excellent way to learn the potency of stillness onstage, to cultivate careful listening. Language is not improvised—the only words that can be spoken are the lines that the dreamer provides from the text. Sounds are encouraged throughout. When the text of the recorded dream is complete, the dreamees freeze and the dreamer has an opportunity to improvise a brief ending to the dream any way he or she wishes.

At the conclusion of the exercise, I ask everyone onstage, "How did it feel?" There's no attempt to analyze the dream; interpretation is only for the dreamer to explore privately. As a group we evaluate the work in terms of acting craft and improvisational technique. How well did the dreamees work together? Did they make strong physical choices? Did they listen? Did they create sound and texture and rhythm? Did they create vivid images from the text/script/dream? Dreamscapes foster kinesthetic awareness in a group. When we've been rehearsing very intensely or are stuck creatively in development process, the practice of embodying a dream will release tension and invigorate our energy. Although it is not an intellectual exercise sometimes after being "inside" the dream, a message will come through for both the dreamer and the dreamees. Dreamscapes encourage trust because you've allowed your fellow company members to play around in your subconscious and mix it up with everyone's various personas.

. . .As the mountain shook lava shot from the top and my nest caught fire, I was shaking with fear and I knew I had to fly. I just jumped and flapped my wings as my parents showed me. I fell a few meters and then I just flew and flew.

The Dream of the Eagle Chick

The Dream of the Eagle Chick touched a chord in all of us. Without ever discussing its meaning, we all knew that Brown Paper Studio was the Eagle Chick gathering courage to fly. Soon we would be soaring.

2005

Safety
Childhood

"Here at the drama we all sit together. . .no matter what color, what kind of hair, we all sit together, what color of the eyes, it doesn't matter. . .the race thing, we didn't have a problem here at the drama class."

Glendale Brown Paper Studio Youth

Right at the start of my first year as a Fulbright scholar, I begin lobbying for my second year. I pay a visit to the U.S. ambassador, Dr. Jendayi Frazer, a distinguished and approachable Black woman, to present my case. When we met in Cape Town at a consulate film screening, she handed me a card with a friendly invitation to contact her. I schedule an appointment at her Pretoria office, and after fifteen minutes of a hardline pitch delivered at my best New York City pace about the brilliance of my innovative program in South Africa, she promptly gets on the telephone and approves another six months of work, allowing me to stay overseas and continue building Brown Paper Studio.

I have to be persistent. I am living on both sides of the world. I am an international artist and educator, stretching my identity as much as my students. I am creating a program where there was none before, making it up as I go along. I get used to seeing the amused expression of "Oh, here she is again" on people's faces when I show up at their offices day after day, week after week, canvassing for supplies, donations, any kind of assistance. I look harmless enough, wearing T-shirts, flip-flops, and faded jeans, carrying sacks of bananas. I am an amiable and total pest, hoofing everywhere on campus, trudging up and down steps, triplicate documents in hand, sending hopeful e-mails, optimistically submitting proposals, making repeated upbeat phone calls, posting flyers, scheduling follow-up appointments, sharing news about Brown Paper Studio with anyone within earshot. I make a point to learn secretaries' names and to greet them with the respect they are due because everyone knows the only way anything happens anywhere in the world is because of secretaries.

D'CIPHER: Set the Record Round is selected to participate in two performances in the 2005 Cape Town Festival, the first at the outdoor event NightVision on famous Long Street, and a Sunday matinee at Artscape, one of the city's major arts venues. The festival is the first time most of my company members are performing in a theater, and for many, one of the few visits to the theater at all. With only limited funds, I am fortunate to hire Mamaki, a marvelous stage manager. She and I must train everyone from the ground up. All the protocols, practices, conventions, and language of the stage are brand new to our company, and in any professional space where time is definitely money, these rituals must be strictly observed. We are in a creative crash course.

At the university our ranks are building every week as we continue to welcome fresh talent to the regularly scheduled Brown Paper Studio sessions on Wednesday and Thursday afternoons. Our hard work is paying off; we've attracted the favorable attention of Professor Brian O'Connell, the university's rector, who generously provides funding as an extracurricular activity. I use the money to buy brown paper, markers, and lots of fruit. I learned from Guga S'Thebe that feeding the company is crucial; even here at the university level, students go hungry, sometimes sitting all day in classes on tea and bread. Brown Paper's tradition of having a big basket of fruit to share freely during breaks remains a key to our success.

It's an accurate aphorism that the best way to really learn something is to teach it. I tell my performing company of about twenty dedicated members that it is time for them to start sharing their creative skills. I ask how they feel about teaching the exercises and games of Brown Paper Studio. No one answers. By now I am accustomed to South African students' natural reserve and formality, in contrast to assertive, highly opinionated American students. After the short silence, there's laughter.

I'm curious. "What's so funny?"

"Well...you see...we're already doing it."

"Really?"

"I use the games in my first-year English tutorials. It helps everyone to focus and settle down. They come on time. They are more productive."

I'm impressed. "Anyone else teaching the games?"

"I do. Helps my Hip Hop collective freestyle. We use them to warm up, loosen up."

I'm thrilled. Company members are taking initiative. Could Brown Paper Studio's simple practices be used to invigorate all areas of education and civic dialogue? By playing and laughing together, can we quickly discover the plans, ideas, concepts, potentials for human development? Is writing on the wall, playing games in a circle, recording dreams, breathing, and singing a way through to the new social systems we so desperately need?

Apparently.

It works because it engages our bodies. The graduate student teacher observed this in her first-year students, the MC knew it enlivened musicians. People concentrate better when they are in their whole body. They are not asked to split, to become just a head, to leave the groin and jaw and limbs behind. This is how the knowledge and awareness actually flows and takes root—through the body.

My company members knew the answers before I even asked. I envision them working in teams of two or three, combining genders, languages, and culture. We would be modeling teamwork and diversity. Facilitating a studio is a huge undertaking and can be overwhelming. We would need a framework.

"Do you all think you can do this, take Brown Paper to the next level?"

Affirmative.

Less than a month after that conversation, I receive a call from HealthWise South Africa in the university's HIV/AIDS office. They are conducting a long-term intervention in the Cape Flats school system to help youth make healthy lifestyle choices. They want an after-school program that will offer alternatives to the lure of gangs, drugs, and violence. Brown Paper Studio's reputation is growing. I jump at the opportunity. When I present the proposal, the company members are so excited, they offer to volunteer. "No way" I interject. "You each spent a year dedicating your time and your energy to developing skills, and they are valuable. Even a small stipend is merited." I want these "soft skills" they acquired to be acknowledged. Too often in South Africa, a professional gathering is full of qualified people who don't know how to communicate with each other. All the answers to all our issues are "already in the room," but without the soft skills that facilitate interpersonal communication, nothing productive can happen. Examples of soft skills are active listening, awareness of breath, patience, honest negotiation, accepting truths different from your own, confidentiality, vulnerability, speaking from the "I," mutual respect, choosing language that fosters cooperation, and a willingness to balance process with product. These are traits associated with the feminine and as such are devalued and taken for granted. These are the qualities my company members have learned and cultivated in the process of making theater. I insist we get paid so they can recognize how, as creativity facilitators, they make it possible for everyone's gifts to be utilized. I also want them to value what they are doing enough to someday consider careers. A budget is created, a date is set for us to begin, and we launch Brown Paper Studio at Glendale Senior Secondary School in Mitchell's Plain.

"Out of drama you get the self-confidence, when you do poems or stories or acting, you will do better than what the other children are doing. You will learn more experience here than what you learn at school."

Glendale Brown Paper Studio Youth

Mitchell's Plain is an area of the Cape Flats designated for Coloured South Africans following the mass forced removals of people classified as nonwhite under apartheid. It is bordered by Khayalestia, the largest Black township in Cape Town, also established under the same brutal conditions. To this day, the lines of division persist. Our Glendale students came from both of these areas. I was adamant that Brown Paper Studio would work in a school that had Black and Coloured students—it was important that we share our process where young people desperately needed to communicate.

"I am talking about the multicultural things and I, yes and me as a person, I wouldn't go to their group because I feel like I wouldn't fit in but now they talking about something and I wouldn't understand, but now when we in drama class we all friends. When they talk about something then we ask them now what does that mean and so we learn their language as well."

Glendale Brown Paper Studio Youth

The Cape Flats in both Black and Coloured areas has severe issues of substance abuse, gangs, unemployment, substandard housing, domestic violence, and inadequate health care. South Africa classifies youth as between the ages of fourteen and thirty-five years. Some 41 percent of Mitchell's Plain is classified as youth. According to statistics from the 2001 census, HealthWise South Africa's report states:

"On average there would be six to eight people living in a two to three bedroom home resulting in overcrowding. Overcrowding in any space essentially leads to overwhelming health and social problems. A small percentage of the community lives in informal settlements...these do not have running water, electricity and toilet facilities."

For the Black students who traveled from Khayalestia, these informal settlements are the norm rather than the exception. Throughout the Cape Flats, almost half of the population's wages are the equivalent of $226 per month. Unemployment runs as high as 78 percent. These are the typical living conditions of our students.

Brown Paper Studio facilitators trek to Glendale twice a week after school for two-and-a-half-hour sessions. We haul rolls of brown paper, markers, a CD player, music, and bags of much appreciated fruit to a big community hall built on the school grounds. The cinderblock building is sweltering in summer and drafty in winter, when we have to work in coats, hats, and gloves. If it is raining, as it often is in Cape Town, the pounding noise on the corrugated metal roof is too loud to hear yourself think, much less speak. The rehearsal hall always needs to be swept of the constant Cape Flats dust, and the bathrooms rarely have toilet paper.

"You can never go with problems and look all sad because when you come, when you talk to them and they like I don't say they make a joke of everything but it's like they kind of take you away from that problem and try to make you feel comfortable and they encourage us a lot."

Glendale Brown Paper Studio Youth

"Make a sound about how you feel" opens every Brown Paper Studio session. We stand in a circle connecting hands. This small gesture of touch is crucial. We relax the body, and then with hands connected, start to twist and turn to make a sound about how we feel. It is a quick diagnostic for the room, and without fail, after a first few sessions, the initially self-conscious facial expressions and inhibited movements give way as the company looks forward to letting go of control. Young people relish making sounds. They scream and squeak and shake themselves up, and in doing so, let go of the first layer of tension and restrictions of the day. They are ridiculously happy just holding hands and making noise. Adults take longer, although not that much. They are afraid of looking silly, and we let them know that's exactly the point. They see that we facilitators are enjoying this absurd, chaotic moment and join in.

Make a sound about how you feel is a hybrid practice, somewhere between the disparate worlds of the Black American field holler as a release of unspeakable pain and an extension of my mentor Allan Miller's technique to coach actors. The shout of Africans in bondage vocalizes unbearable loss—at the same time, it is a call for freedom, for the ecstasy of liberation. In acting training, making a sound keeps you connected to the truth of you in the moment, it gives texture to the text. Our opening ritual in Brown Paper Studio combines a fundamental Black musical concept with a pragmatic technique from my training and experience as a performer.

Make a sound about how you feel seems like a throwaway moment. We start making sound before we start talking, and it's effective because no one thinks too much about it. Howling and shouting together while moving unlocks the tough spaces of the body. As facilitators, we can feel the energy shift enough for us to ease in and start to massage the room, coax it into self-expression. Most people want to chatter or make nervous jokes before making a sound. Making a sound is primal, naked, exposed, funky—so we'd rather cover these sounds up with meaningless words, verbal masks. That's why we always begin with making a sound about how you feel. It's where we begin at Glendale.

I also learned something at drama class that I never knew...I never had patience with anything, and here I had to have patience because we busy with rehearsals and now we doing the play and someone does something wrong, we have to wait, do some all over, stuff like that and you have to have patience...ask us we know.

Glendale Brown Paper Studio Youth

At this point I must formulate the Brown Paper Basics so that my company members have a teaching template. I distill several themes that distinguish my process: Be On Time, Gratitude, Safety, Circle, Breath, Eye Contact, and Trust. I find it both humorous and revealing that I've organized my methodology into seven basics, a bit like the Nguzo Saba, also known as the Seven Principles of Kwanzaa created in the 1960s as part of Black Nationalist culture.

These Basics are touchstones. They are what ground us, bring us into being present. Each one has a physical, emotional, mental, and spiritual expression. They are organized in a specific order based on how we unfold as individuals and as a group. The Basics came from my decades of practice as a theater artist. They did not come from my head, they came from my belly. Over and over I've tested what wakes people up, what opens them wide, what takes them deep, what brings them alive. I've collected techniques that allow us to have more of ourselves, because that's what we all want, more of ourselves. Trust is last on the list—it can also be considered first, because it's the moment when you say yes to yourself. Your loud and clear "yes" is what gets you into the studio and what brings you back.

The Glendale students arrive, hiding their nervousness by being boisterous or by huddling together in curious silence. There are talent shows in Mitchell's Plain, an after-school drama class is something new. They play games. They are introduced to the Basics. They are taught how to prepare the room by clearing away chairs, sweeping the hall, posting brown paper on the wall, making the empty space into an orderly and pleasant studio for our sessions. They are called actors, they must come to every rehearsal on time, they must learn their lines, learn choreography, learn cues for entrances and exits. They must be patient and encouraging and disciplined. They are now part of a company. After four months of our nurturing boot camp, Glendale Brown Paper Studio is ready for its first show, *Looking for Mike.* The play is funny and ingenious. It was written by one of my graduate students in Memory & Vision and can accommodate a big company. A perfect fit. To cast roles, we hold "auditions." These are really an opportunity for every young actor to get a taste of the pressure of being onstage in front of an audience. Teachers and counselors are amazed that regardless of their mother tongue—Xhosa, Afrikaans, or English—every student chooses to read for a part. As is the custom in Brown Paper, every student who participates in the after-school training is in the play. With only one exception, a young woman who had to leave for the Eastern Cape with her family before the end of the school year, every student who read at the auditions stands holding hands onstage at the final show's curtain call.

"Here at Brown Paper, the facilitators they are friends and it is easier to work with them because there is a friendship, mutual respect. Everything is there."

Glendale Brown Paper Studio Youth

Almost half the students who came to us in the first weeks of our residency at Glendale stayed with us for four years, through their entire high school experience. The Glendale Brown Paper Studio company met as teenagers when they were forming a social identity. In the process of making theater, they learned each other's names and then some of each other's language and culture. They dared to be an alternative culture in a segregated high school environment. They discovered their own definition of what it means to be South African. Company membership was based entirely on one's participation: if you showed up, engaged fully, worked hard, and played hard, you were part of Brown Paper Studio. Being chosen meant choosing your self.

A heavy-set boy with a guarded expression comes into the circle, standing stiff and awkward in his overcoat. He is Coloured, with mahogany eyes and curly black hair, and underneath his pudgy boyishness, you can see a handsome young man will emerge. He reminds me of Salim at that age.

"You can leave your coat over on the chair," suggests a Brown Paper facilitator.

"I'm keeping it on."

"You'll be more comfortable playing the games." The facilitator's coaching is gentle.

"I'm not playing today."

"We need you to participate if you want to be in the circle. We'd like you to stay."

It's a Brown Paper Studio requirement that everyone in the room, even adult visitors who are there to observe, must at least join the warm-up.

"I'm keeping my coat on." Our invitation has been accepted. The shy boy wears his overcoat for the first few weeks. After graduation—matric, as it is called in South Africa—he goes to varsity to become a theater director.

Another boy, small, quick, and wiry, incessantly asks me questions that begin with "Miss…" His thick Capetonian accent makes it sound like "Muss." Hardly ever still, to the point of being disruptive, in the States he would be medicated for hyperactivity. A wonderful performer, he learns the warm-ups instantly—having played a game only once, he can teach it perfectly. He comes from a large Muslim family, always wears his kofi hat, and sometimes brings one of his younger siblings to rehearsal. "Muss, did you know when I came to Brown Paper I was getting ready to join a gang? If I had not come here, by now I could have been dead."

A lanky Black girl speaks so softly she cannot be heard in normal conversation; sometimes she just nods or shakes her head yes or no, rather than speak. She wears her hair in a short, tight ponytail of stiffly straightened hair. She misses nothing, even though her eyes are slightly downcast. Once she gets onstage to perform in *Looking for Mike,* there is no longer any problem hearing her. She takes the spotlight with a big voice. By the next year, she assumes the responsibility of Glendale Brown Paper company manager. When she is in her senior year of high school, she looks the school principal full in the eye and advocates for the program to continue: "I am who I am because of Brown Paper Studio."

"I learnt how to do things, how to do the things on my own, learnt to stand on my own two feet."

Glendale Brown Paper Studio Youth

At the same time we are producing *Looking for Mike,* Hanan visits me in South Africa for six weeks. My dear daughter is a Pisces. Her element is the ocean, and even here in Cape Town her bedroom is an underwater landscape, everything is everywhere floating in a chaotic soup that only she comprehends. Hanan's spirit is vast like the ocean; she can manage all sorts of divergent personalities with ease. People are comfortable with her, they often confide in her, sensing her innate compassion. The Brown Paper company of facilitators and students warms to her immediately.

Hanan has always taken her time waking up, slowly rising from the sea floor, not quite fully awake until coffee and her first cigarette complete the daily metamorphosis from mermaid to human. When she surfaces, generally sometime around noon, I hear bracelets jangling in her private aquarium. She swims in a limbo state for twenty minutes or so, until armed with caffeine and nicotine, she's now ready to communicate and on this particular day, is poised to confront her mother's folly. Despite her own love affair with Cape Town and Brown Paper

Studio, Hanan sits me down for the interrogation: "What are you trying to prove? Why are you working long hours in a hot, grimy hall on the edge of the ghetto with so little support? How are you going to get this raggedy-ass show ready to open in a few days?" I listen. Hanan's honest opinion is often a litmus test for my projects. It's clear she's fed up with my low-paying dedication, my endless cycles of overdrive and invisibility. My daughter is afraid I will fail and my intense efforts will look pathetic. "Watch, sweetheart," I assure her. "The same magic of the theater you have seen many times before you will see again. Just watch." In Pisces fashion, she lets go of judgment and doesn't mention her concern again. After the show, when the Glendale actors come offstage hugging and shouting and literally jumping with joy, Hanan breaks down sobbing. She experiences her ecstatic moment, the feeling that overwhelmed me backstage after the first show at Guga S'Thebe in 2002. Having been a youth advocate since she herself was in high school, her relieved, elated postshow tears strengthen an already deep commitment to her after-school program when she returns to the States. She understands this is the payoff, the self-love and self-esteem that make it all worthwhile.

"Because they believe in us and that's why we believe in ourselves."

Glendale Brown Paper Studio Youth

Did we argue, Medi and I?

Oh yes.

About what?

The Cars.

From the beginning of our love affair, Medi wanted me to buy a car, and as I needed something to get around town, I agreed. Footballers are all about style, so he convinced me to get a used BMW. They are everywhere in South Africa. I do believe they are the worst cars in the world. The joke about BMW being an abbreviation for Bring Money With is not a joke. Eventually I realized the ones I bought were built during the early '90s, the Ungovernable Years, and no doubt assembled by disgruntled autoworkers who sabotaged these overpriced rich-people's luxury vehicles with *muti*, a term for malevolent witchcraft, or if not evil spells, at least really bad vibes.

The first car was a little white piece of shit that I quickly sold to purchase an even more worthless cream-colored piece of shit. The absolute worst part was that I sold the first car without consulting my partner. Any sensible woman knows this is *verboten*; never come between a man and his car, and even if he agrees to the transaction, let him do the business. I didn't, which was the genesis of some serious trust issues compounded by my mounting paranoia about being an older woman used for her money. The car became a flashpoint that tainted many of our interactions. So we quarreled, me mostly ranting and raving, while he steadily withdrew.

That second BMW was almost Medi's coffin. Driving too fast at night around a corner on the mountain, he slammed into the back of a pickup truck. Both vehicles spun, and he was hit again on the side. The truck was barely dented, our car was mostly wrecked, and Medi was knocked out of his body in fear. He arrives home in the mangled, demonic BMW, disoriented and distraught. "I almost died," is all he can say.

I am not hearing it. I am livid. "How could you? You rear-ended them! Why were you speeding? You're at fault. We have no insurance coverage. I can't afford more repairs. I can't afford I can't afford I can't afford..." He is sitting on the curb looking bewildered, looking back and forth between me and the car, still stunned. "I almost died," he repeats.

Pissed, I stamp into the house, righteously indignant that once again he's become a liability. Both of us need to cry. We don't. Later that night we lie in bed saying nothing. The air is brittle until somewhere in this awful eternity, he touches me and kisses me and pulls me close. Always hard to resist him, I yield and sense there is more happening here than our favorite dance of seduction. His being inside me is the way back into his own body. I become the earth, his strokes let him affirm he is still alive, that he miraculously walked away from a near-fatal auto crash. My heart submits to his sheer gratitude for life as we are moved to tears. That night is more than lovemaking, it is conception, birth, death, and resurrection. A broken car becomes something for tomorrow...and as Medi taught me, although it took years for my compulsive American mind to learn this...tomorrow is another day.

Too much changes when Medi's sister arrives from Congo. I am demoted to second-class family. In keeping with tradition, as her brother, even a younger brother, he is responsible for his sister's well-being in South Africa. He doesn't come around for dinner. Nights with me are no longer a priority. He is even more tired and hassled than ever. Until his sister learns enough English to function and find employment in

South Africa, he must find a way to support two people when he was barely managing one. From her I begin to feel an unspoken expectation that I should be doing more for their household. After all I am a rich American, I live in the white part of town, I work at the university, I have a car that my boyfriend, her brother, drives. I travel back and forth to the United States. I am privileged, period. I am annoyed at my implied responsibilities - nagging my demands into his one ear, while his sister complains into the other.

Unexpectedly I get a glimpse into their ravaged past when Medi suggests, "Let's go to the cinema to see *Hotel Rwanda*." It is an unusual request as our only dates are generally free soccer games. The movie has just been released in South Africa. I am curious how such a catastrophic event is handled on film, plus I'm a big fan of Don Cheadle.

"I was in Rwanda," Medi continues. "I was there in the fighting, in the war."

I'm sure he means he has been in the same places where the fighting and the genocide occurred. With a slightly condescending edge, I correct him, saying "Not *during* the civil war, that's not what you mean."

"I'm telling you I was there; I lived in Kigali when the war started."

He is lying, I think to myself, *or he still doesn't understand my question.* "Come on, Medi." My attitude is suspect. "You were in Rwanda during the genocide?" He recognizes my disbelief and in a matter-of-fact tone begins his story.

"It was in April, a semifinal game of the African Cup. Nigeria was playing Cote D'Ivoire. I was at my friend Emanuel's house watching the match on TV. At ten p.m. the announcement comes on that the president is dead; his plane has been shot down. About two hours later, all the lights go out, and at two a.m. the shooting begins. When I get to my house, we have to sleep on mattresses in the hallway so the bullets don't hit us. In the houses on both sides, I hear the people being killed, whole families crying and screaming. We have to stay there for a week, and then my father, who works for the Red Cross, gets permission for us to leave. On the way to the airport, our van is pulled over and the soldiers make my sister get out. They say she is Tutsi. She will be shot in the head. My father shows him his official Red Cross identification. He says, 'If you plan to kill her you must kill me first.' They let us drive on to the airport."

The night after his sister's arrival we are sitting in a cafe having a drink, and out of the blue, she corroborates the story, describing how close she came to being executed. Her English is sparse; her brother translates. "They were going to shoot me. They put the gun to my head. I thought I was no more." With pride she turns to look at her brother and then looks back at me. "You know, Medi is such a great player. The Belgian and the Spanish coaches come by our house every day after school. They wanted to take him from Kinshasa to Europe. They wanted him for their leagues, to play for them. My father says no, he cannot go. My father says he is too young to leave Africa. So me and Medi go to Rwanda to be close to my father where he works. That is why we are there when the war begins. We see it all."

How can I be so selfish? This young widow, who has already been through two holocausts, first Rwanda and now DRC, has just had to leave her country and her small daughter behind. She is fleeing a situation so awful no one really talks about it. Am I that callous? Am I the same as the oblivious Americans that I ridicule? In comparison, what do I have to gripe about?

I feel guilty and torn, and truth be told I need more. I'm helping to support them both, and I'm still I'm not getting what I want. Guilt is an utterly useless emotion unless it moves you to make a decision. When guilt rears its grisly head, you know it's time to either accept whatever happened, make peace, and forgive yourself, or to take action that deals with the issue at hand. Often both strategies are necessary, otherwise guilt will eat you alive. I was already feeling guilty for living well in South Africa; the discomfort did not start with Medi and his sister. I cautioned Salim when he came to Cape Town to put away his camera, iPod, computer, and headphones when people visited. I could see their reaction to so many valuable items lying casually around the house. It made us look rich, and relative to many of our guests, we were. What an irony—in the States I worked overtime to make sure we did not look shabby. Due to the pernicious hoax of television, the world believes that everyone in the States has wealth and access to celebrity, that we are literally The Bold and the Beautiful. A bright, young Angolan man once asked me how Whitney and Bobby were doing, as though they were my neighbors; a South African woman who attended Brown Paper Studio wanted to know if I see Denzel on the street; and an older South African man who worked at our local grocery store commented wistfully one morning that everyone in America "smiles a lot and seems very happy." Mindless media-induced mirages aside, as U.S. citizens we obviously do have economic advantages that are unheard of for the overwhelming majority of African people.

"I want to eat meat, we never have meat," Medi's sister tells me as her English improves. She expects me to buy it for her, and why not? I can afford it. I get mad because I don't want to, and then I see myself as greedy. Then I get mad because although I really can't support three households, I want to see myself as generous. When I acquiesce and say yes, I end up being resentful, and when I say no, I feel I must hide my assets. These constant tensions create two camps Medi must live between, a dichotomy that erodes our relationship. In Africa blood family is always first and I guess in African America, too, since my children and my aged mother are my priority.

Publicly Medi and I are status quo; privately we are turning sour. At this point nothing he does is enough. Despite our stormy weather, he treats my party-girl daughter with the utmost kindness and considera-tion. He cordially chauffeurs her day and night and keeps a watchful eye on her cavorting around Cape Town. He is as protective as he would be for any family member of his own, he treats her just the way he has always cared for my son. Fed up with guilt and an absentee lover, my eyes start roving, looking for someone who can give me the time and attention I deserve.

Back at the university, we are preparing for our part in Centre for the Performing Arts' end-of-the-year concert. I need to create another performance piece for a large cast of sixteen people and decide to adapt a classic children's book, *John Brown, Rose & the Midnight Cat*, using lots of movement, no props, and a traditional Greek-style chorus. Brown Paper

Studio is producing two large shows at the same time on a nonexistent budget. The obvious stresses aside, I feel increasingly more welcome in South Africa than in the States. Each time I return to New York, the oppressive paranoia of the Bush regime is more palpable. The rich are getting richer, and the poor are getting sent to war and prison in ever increasing numbers. On school playgrounds, our children are emulating our bullying behavior in the world. Reality TV is gaining popularity as the American people become more delusional, strung out on pharmaceutical drugs with side effects more deadly than the ailments. Every magazine stand projects a hypnotic display of the same perfectly bland white face over and over, a Jim Crow media conspiracy to make me believe that these fake celebrities have actually done something worthwhile to merit my attention. We know the names of clothing designers and don't know our neighbors. Hurricane Katrina spirals from a natural disaster into ethnic cleansing. The United States has sold its soul for bigger SUVs and smaller cell phones. Homeland Insecurity greets me at JFK International Airport with a red digital sign scrolling "God Bless America."

By contrast, in the world of Brown Paper Studio, I too am "connecting first to myself and then to other people," to my growing community of students, artists, company members, and friends who have become an extended family.

Invariably on both sides of the Atlantic, my students will come to me and say, "My parents don't want me to go into the arts; they think I ought to have something to fall back on."

"Fine," I answer, "although I can't help you with that. I know about choosing the life of the artist, accepting that your art form—in this case theater—has chosen you. Committing to that choice and living with the conviction that you have an absolute right to express your talent and make a good living. After all, somebody's going to succeed—why not you? Don't you have a right to happiness and fulfillment?" For a number of my students, South African and North American, I am the only person who says it's possible. I am their sole advocate for an artistic life.

My parents gave me the freedom to be an artist. They never questioned my choice to be a performer. When my students hear supportive words coming from my mouth, it is my parents' voice they are hearing. My mother was a jazz vocalist who would have had a fine career if my father had not insisted that she choose between marriage and The Road. Born and raised in Harlem, my father knew the streets, he knew clubs and cabarets, he knew bars and hangouts, and he wasn't too keen on my beautiful and talented mother traveling for weeks in a bus with hep-cat musicians. My father had his own brand of innovation—in the early 1960s, he bought a super 8 mm movie camera and documented the lives of his family and his friends. He knew we were making history. Growing up, my mother and father were surrounded by gifted Black people, some who became celebrities and some who kept their day jobs while continuing to paint or make music or act or write. Harlem is one of the cultural capitals of the world. I applaud my soul for choosing to incarnate in the midst of its extraordinary artistry and style.

My parents gave me New York City - I am a proud second generation New Yorker. I've either lived, attended school, worked or had boyfriends in Harlem, the Upper West Side, the Upper East Side, the Lower East

Side, Greenwich Village, Chelsea, Midtown, and Brooklyn's Fort Greene and Brownsville sections. Our family went to museums, galleries, outdoor art exhibits, concerts, movies, theater, ballet, and modern dance. We dined uptown and downtown at fine restaurants. We enjoyed French and Italian cuisine, Jewish delicatessen food, Harlem rotisserie chicken, and Chinese takeout. Early on Sunday mornings when the streets were quiet from the previous night's revelry and the churchgoers were not yet out in full force, my daddy would drive us all over Manhattan in his trendsetting foreign cars. Before European imports were status among Black people, he owned one of the first Volvos in the United States. We rode around admiring architecture, noting changes in the skyline, observing how neighborhoods had shifted their borders. We appreciated our famous hometown, in my father's words "the greatest city in the world."

My parents gave me a knack for hospitality. They threw great parties with interesting people, plenty of top-shelf liquor and fabulous home-cooked food. My folks were salespeople; Daddy sold whiskey to Harlem stores and bars. Mom was a pioneer in New York's garment district, going into business and founding the first Black-owned haute couture fashion house. Other than our bountiful welcome table and well-stocked bar, our lifestyle was quite ordinary, almost white bread, like fake brown bread that's bleached flour with a bit of food coloring. In the blandness of desegregation, it's best to fit in, to assimilate, so in the predictability of our home, I became a Drama Queen. To break the humdrum of mid-twentieth century America's Melmac plastic plates, TV game shows, stifling Eisenhower administration, and cumbersome garter belts, I invented myself as a stage director. As the adults drank

Johnnie Walker Red and Jack Daniels on the rocks, gossiped, discussed uptown and international politics in the living room, I created the Blue Fairy stories with the children of our close family friends. Rather a quiet child, when it came to theater, I was quite bossy. I always cast myself as The Beautiful Princess and the oldest brother as My Handsome Prince. His big sister got to play the Evil Witch, and with the other kids, I created a supporting cast for my personal myth. At some point in the evening when the parents were sufficiently tipsy, I'd come out to announce it was time for the show. They always went along with the program, giving us a big round of applause as we took our bows. At home in my room, I created cutting-edge karaoke, dragging out recordings of musicals and lip-syncing or singing along to *My Fair Lady* or *Carousel,* and performed my own sketches to Ella Fitzgerald's "Mack the Knife." My parents sat patiently, maintaining a straight face while their odd little Negro girl-child acted out the entire soundtracks of *The King and I* or *West Side Story.* Is there any way to adequately thank them other than to wholeheartedly encourage my students?

My parents gave me Martha's Vineyard. The Island has been my longest, steadiest love affair. I am six years old when we arrive at night after being on the road winding through New England for what seems like forever. We pause at someplace called Woods Hole, drive up a ramp into the brightly lit mouth of the *Islander* ferry. The boat ploughs through water that is silver black and endless until we dock at a wooden pier on this faraway shore. Even though it's very late, we children are allowed to walk down the beach road. The streetlights are little moons. The air smells like adventure, and a thin shroud of fog makes it all the more mysterious. We walk close together, shy at the silence and a sky without limits. Although I didn't know such a world existed, the dark expanse of ocean feels like something I have always wanted. In the sunshine of the next morning, we set out to explore our heaven. Imagine, after living in the gray tension of New York, being able to walk outside barefoot. Imagine seeing Black people tending their rose and hydragena bushes, playing tennis in neat white skirts and belted shorts, strolling to the beach, cooking supper on the grill, sitting out on the porch with nothing to do other than to sip cocktails while the sun goes down. Imagine the curve of an unbroken horizon. The Island lets us know we are on top of the world.

I remember 1960s department stores had a unique clothing size: 6X, "X" as in "extra." I loathed shopping those racks. I had a pot belly, thick thighs, chubby cheeks. I was pigeon-toed, with an untamed head of hair and blue-speckled kitty-cat eyeglasses. I was born with a weak left eye. I had to undergo surgery to keep the left eye from crossing. That's all I needed—to be cockeyed—and the trauma about my physical appearance would have been complete. Like an ugly duckling turning into a swan, one miraculous summer at camp, I lost my tenacious baby fat. I came home with curves where before there were rolls. I was thirteen and foxy. My new figure blossomed just in time, because throughout the known universe, nothing could possibly be any better than being a Black teenager on Martha's Vineyard in the 1960s. *Say it Loud, I'm Black and I'm Proud,* and I'm beautiful and I'm spending the summer on one of the most idyllic island resorts in the world with a whole bunch of equally good-looking young people who are convinced the planet now belongs to them.

We are as unexpected and unstoppable as Black America herself. We wear Afros and bikinis and dashikis. We eat fried clams and lobster, boogaloo and shingaling to the latest Motown hits, play bid whist and blackjack, make out, make noise, and walk tall. We swim naked in the brisk Gay Head surf and smear our pretty brown bodies with red clay from the cliffs. "We Got More Soul" with Dyke and the Blazers at house-party porches strung with colored lights, as we smoke reefer, drink cheap wine, and wake up the next morning passed out on the front lawn with our first hangovers. We are the children of doctors and salespeople and lawyers and librarians and postal workers and nurses and politicians and teachers and hustlers and judges. The Vineyard is not yet the glamorous destination of movie stars and presidents. Oak Bluffs is still a sleepy fishing harbor, and Edgartown remains off-limits to Black people, except for those "in service" as maids and cooks. We claim solidarity with all oppressed people, while we ride around with our convertible tops down under the dazzling Vineyard sun.

My parents gave me Africa. They planted the seeds of cultural exchange and pan-African consciousness early. In the 1950s my mother hosted a luncheon for the ambassador from the newly independent nation of Ghana and his entourage as part of her volunteer work with the United Nations. For years she kept in touch with these distinguished men, who enjoyed the hospitality of "a regular American family" and who she described "as so warm and down to earth."

My brother, George, and I are descendants of our paternal grandmother, an immigrant from the West Indies, who marched on Seventh Avenue in Marcus Garvey's "Back to Africa" parades in the early twentieth century. George served as an Episcopal priest in Botswana in the

'80s and was involved with South African activism during the struggle years. When I was planning my first trip in 2002, he gave me money to travel, saying, "Everyone must go to South Africa."

My father was a self-educated man, and as such he wanted to investigate what was happening on the Continent for himself. Books of Mandela's writings arrived in the mail from the United Kingdom because they weren't for sale in the States. Every Christmas morning as we opened our own presents, we would all stop and watch Daddy unpack his favorite gift, some newly released, hardback, first-edition book on Black history. He would smile and hold it, turning it over and over, marveling at its weight, its binding, its beauty. For him, it was a work of art. After we had coffee and hot chocolate and pastry, my father would retire to his easy chair, open his new book and transport himself, only coming back to share a tidbit of information or his opening line for a particularly meaningful story, "You know I never realized..." We would marvel at him, sitting and reading his new book from cover to cover, sometimes in one day.

On this winter's evening in 1961, I hear my father's footsteps fall slowly as he climbs the stairs at the end of his workday. He has the saddest look I've ever seen on his face and sits down heavily in a living-room chair. When he addresses my mother, his voice is numb.

"Lillian, they killed Lumumba."

My father is not only grieving the assassination of Patrice Emery Lumumba, the Republic of Congo's recently democratically elected prime minister, my father is mourning his hope for a free and unified Africa. Something precious has been lost, something of great value is broken. Every Black child learns too early how to read the messages in their parents' hushed or furious tones, in their caged body language, in their fractured gaze. We little ones are not allowed to be innocent, this monster is too dangerous. We must remember that "it" is always right outside the door, and on this evening "it" has invaded our home because our parents are now talking about "it". The specter of white world supremacy contorts the room.

"Lillian, they killed Lumumba."

From then on, if I was giggling too much in school or if I wanted to stop acting silly, I would think about Daddy's footsteps and expression and voice. Remembering his somber words would make me sit still and be serious. Without realizing it, that night I inherited my father's dream of African liberation.

My parents gave me courage. Safety is high on the list of Brown Paper Basics. I am committed to creating safe spaces because being in a Black female body can be very unsafe. Any girl's body learns too early it is a target. If the body has dark skin, it is all the more susceptible to violence. A world defined by sex and race resents the fact that you have a vagina—even your small one represents too much power. Being desirable makes you a threat. You are bombarded by church and state with the message "Don't trust your body, it is evil and will betray you." The violation of the feminine is so pervasive that no family has been spared. Everyone suffers, women and men alike.

It's important to emphasize that Brown Paper Studio is not drama therapy; if facilitators suspect a participant has experienced trauma or abuse, we must refer that person to an appropriate professional for attention. What we do ask is for people to peel back layers of armor to expose the soft underbelly of their childlike self. Without habitual defenses, we can allow ourselves to be more playful, and paradoxically we are then more stable. True creativity and innovation can happen if the human being feels she or he will be valued for her or his contribution. People who go through the process become "full of themselves." They recognize "I am worthwhile and I have something to offer." If Brown Paper Studio has done anything for its participants, it has set a very high standard for how they expect to be treated.

Young, old, male, female, every color and size and shape, we all deserve to be totally and completely safe in our body. A safe space is one where you can trust your feelings, your intuition, your gut. It is a space where you can be heard and respected, where you can integrate your physical, emotional, mental, and spiritual selves. Your spiritual self is the part that never forgets its connection to the whole. Your spiritual self knows Unity.

My parents gave me spiritual integrity. As a young girl, I came home from Sunday school, walked into the kitchen, and flat out told my mother, "I don't believe those stories." I was uncomfortable praying to a crucified savior. Looking up at the thorns and blood and anguished face disturbed me. Not missing a beat, she replied, "You don't have to go back." Her decision altered the shape of my life. I didn't really have to worship anything. My mother was a member of the Socialist Party in the 1940s, drawn to politics with no particular allegiance to religion. Her faith was a private matter. Church was about fellowship, about interacting with the people of the congregation, and my mother truly loved people. Although she was highly opinionated, I never heard her speak on behalf of God or Jesus, suggesting what they might want or might not want for me. I was born into a Christian family, attended school with a large Jewish student body, practiced Buddhist meditation since my teens, married a Muslim man, and in keeping with pagan traditions, navigate my life according to the phases of the moon and the cycles of the sun. My mother gave me permission to write my own creation myth. Her beloved sister, my wise Aunt Jacqueline, counseled me early in life. "Judyie, do you know what it means to be spiritual?" I shook my head no. "Being spiritual is simple, it means being honest."

2006

Circle
Education

The whole town's laughing at me...

Teddy Pendergrass

I hear Medi's tekkies, South African for what we call sneakers in the States, sloshing down the hall. It's full of water where I have been throwing a drunken tantrum in the bathtub, crying and howling in my empty apartment: "You don't give a fuck...you don't love me anyway... I've had it...fuck you, motherfucker." Who knows what the neighbors are thinking?

"What is this?" Medi calls out coming into the house, wading through the water that has overflowed out of the bathroom down to the front door. I start hollering, "What the fuck do you care? You're not here anyway! I'm alone again! I'm by myself again, wah, wah, wah!...," all the while slapping my arms and legs in the water creating a bigger mess. "Ach, Judyie." He's actually cracking up at my antics! Defiantly I make the water more turbulent. Laughing all the way, he goes to get a big towel, grabs me under my arms, and hoists me out of the tub. I'm still sobbing and fussing and wailing, until his firm touch calms me like the infant I have become.

"Relax. I am right here." He dries me off and puts on my bathrobe. I'm doing a version of the posthysterics hiccupping that babies do as he walks me to the bedroom, slides me into the bed, and pulls the covers up to my chin. Chuckling to himself, he gets the mop and pail to clean up. Medi calls this sort of behavior "heart pressure," and according to him, "It is normal for woman." When he finishes his chore, he comes in and as usual turns on the TV to some inane late-night movie, gets in the bed, and slow and steady makes me his baby for real. As I become the center of his universe, my heart pressure is relieved.

Mercifully the TV has died for the night, our darkened space is silent. Before we drift off in our bedroom cocoon, we murmur back and forth to each other. I ask him:

"What do you love about me?...what's special about me?...am I beautiful to you?...when you think about me, what do you think about?... are you happy we're together?...do you get tired of me asking you fifty questions all the time?"

"No," he says, "I get tired of you asking me the same question fifty times. Now sleep."

Judyie, what the hell are you doing? You sorry-assed broad with yet another man too many years younger, who ain't got no steady job, no steady cash, and mouths to feed in South Africa and Congo? I've provided money for his brother's school fees, his sister's beer, his mother's medicine, his rent, his passport, his soccer boots, his hospital fees, money to bail him out of jail for the crime of asserting his civil rights, to feed him, clothe him, and put a roof over his head. Not to mention my loving arms to sleep in. What do you get? Really? A man most times too exhausted from a day of honing his survival skills that he barely has energy for you. Someone so beat down, what could they possibly have to offer? A smile? Kind words? Some fleeting tenderness before he falls out facedown, bone tired? Is that all you are worth, Girlfriend? Don't you even rate a man with a bank account and his own car rolling down the road to success toward a future? "The whole town's laughing at me," croons Teddy Pendergrass, and I know he's singing my tune, too.

I begin to date age-appropriate men living in Cape Town or New York. They take me out for lovely dinners, first-run movies, scenic car rides, champagne brunches—all the nice things a girl wants, needs, and deserves. I get lost in my own maze of self-deception, hoping each new suitor will be the one to break the spell, and hoping even more that he will not. When I get home from these legitimate dates, I am relieved they are over and I don't have to make conversation or pretend to care about what these socially approved escorts are talking about. If I come home sufficiently drunk, I talk to the mirror and pretend it's Medi. I crave his few well-chosen words, his hilarious stories from life on the streets, his spot-on commentary on football and politics. I crave the essence of him, the smell of him, his subtle presence. I crave him, because with him silence is enough.

When I mention Medi to my girlfriends, I can see their eyes go flat with impatience. "Enough of your little fling," they want to say. "You're living at a precipice with phantom income on two continents, an elderly parent, children in college, and needs of your own. He'll float forever and you are left holding the bag. The same trick bag you jumped into at the beginning of this played-out South African adventure. Haven't you learned anything?" The expression on their faces is final, as though someone has just pulled down the window shade and closed the blinds.

With my tempestuous love affair as a backdrop, Brown Paper Studio's development is phenomenal. By borrowing money, I just make it back to Cape Town five days before we are scheduled to open two one-act plays, *Six Thousand Miles* and *Naming Names,* written by company members, at Artscape for our second year in the Cape Town Festival. After the success of *Looking for Mike,* we are firmly established as an after-school program at Glendale Senior Secondary. We are preparing to open another studio as the theater-company-in-residence at Azaad Youth Services, a newly created social-welfare program in District Six. I have no stable income and no health care. When I do get paid, it's in South African rand, seven rand equaling one U.S. dollar, never mind the fact that my bills back home are in U.S. dollars. Before I was able to figure out which friends could loan me enough cash to buy a plane ticket, I wrote to the company:

Dear Brown Paper,

Here I am in New York, very focused on returning to Cape Town as soon as possible. My delays are purely financial and as soon as resources are available, I'll be on a plane. I've been in e-mail communication with a few folks and wanted to update everyone on some ideas, thoughts, plans, and possibilities. . .

Who are we? Where are we going? Why? How? These are important questions, and I know they are on people's mind and heart. Mine too. Please remember we have made it up as we went along and that is the nature of innovation. No one has necessarily done it like this before and so we have to: 1) Breathe 2) Be Creative 3) Trust the Process.

We are a Big Company—everyone who has participated in shows and projects over the past two years plus Glendale. We are in Germany, Norway, the US, the UK and more. We are ALL Brown Paper Studio. We are creating a big vision that has been birthed in South Africa, and it is time for clarity and self-definition even as we expand. Put your thoughts, impressions, ideas, questions, frustrations, epiphanies, and jokes in your journals (remember those?). We will find time to paint the Big Picture. I have confidence in each and every one of you and I am grateful for your hard work, faith, good humor, and brilliance. Keep Breathing!

I Love You,

Judyie

Who are these people I call The Company?

We have talents, issues, histories, skills, idiosyncrasies, gifts, neuroses, genius.

We have short hair, nappy hair, brown, black, and blond hair, dreadlocks, long hair, curls, conks, braids, dyed hair, Mohawks, and ponytails.

We are black, pink, brown, red, white, yellow.

We are Gold.

We are round and sleek and squat and tall and stacked and skinny.

We have big asses and small ones.

We speak lots of languages, code switching is our mother tongue.

We are many religions and various beliefs.

We are All Faith.

We are free enough to be in love across color lines.

We are brave enough to be in love across gender boundaries.

We are partnered and solo.

We have babies, we are growing families.

We suffer tragedy, the loss of one of our precious children, a young son whose elusive smile lives inside us forever.

We share secrets, tell lies, get angry, fall out with each other, and won't speak until we remember it's All Love Anyway.

We are accountants who are novelists, biologists who come alive being onstage, social workers who can do stand-up comedy, addicts who leave behind a life on the streets to reinvent themselves as artists, runaways from the corporate monster who discover they are cultural activists, anthropologists who passionately build community.

We are contradictions and commitment.

We get discouraged, frustrated, pissed off at a world that can't keep up with us.

We leave Brown Paper overworked, underpaid, and after a few months or years of slavery for the machine, we reappear at the door of the studio that is always open, and we are always happy to see whoever returns because it reminds us all why we are crazy enough to stay, hauling fruit and brown paper and making a sound and writing scripts so that people who were invisible can celebrate themselves.

We celebrate ourselves.

We are complex, diverse, and for us identity is a verb.

We are refugees making Bob Marley's *Exodus* from an old world into the New.

We are deep-rooted celestial soul sisters and brothers.

We recognize each other by our vision.

Being a company member means you made it through a Brown Paper Studio show to the curtain call as part of an ensemble.

Every show starts with the Circle.

The Circle sends a message to the psyche that sacred space is being created, a place to tell our individual and collective stories.

The Circle is the sun and the moon and the earth, the big round cycles of cosmic time.

The Circle is a symbol of the whole integrated human being, we replicate that wholeness when we form a circle with our bodies: our chests are open, our breath expands, our hearts are exposed.

The Circle is where we are on the same level, we stand eye to eye, shoulder to shoulder.

The Circle comes after the ground rules of safety are set. In the circle we touch, we hold each other's hands.

The Circle symbolizes Home, we are reassured that we belong.

The spirit of the Circle never leaves. Each time we gather to begin a new show or a new project, I tell company members, novices and veterans alike:

"Even though we may no longer be physically standing in a circle, this feeling exists for you in your performance, this is the support you will feel onstage in a way that lets us know the Circle is unbroken."

The Circle and all of the Brown Paper Basics were codified when I had to find a sustainable system for the UWC college students to teach the Glendale high school students. For over a year now, I've been watching them work together, and I'm convinced that Brown Paper Studio's greatest contribution will be in the arena of public education. As recipients of government funding, HealthWise is required to conduct an objective third-party evaluation by social service professionals at the end of the school year. When I read the report, it is evident that what I'm seeing with my own eyes is being confirmed by educators who bear witness to the success of Brown Paper Studio.

My whole being starts singing, "This is it! This is what I have been looking for!"

In terms of the learners you just see how they have benefited, how they have grown, how vocal they have become, how creative they have become and that sense of developing self within adolescence.

Glendale Educator

There are three simple, straightforward reasons why Brown Paper succeeds in education. Number one is the fact that young people's learning software long ago outstripped the schools, it's akin to putting a new high-speed program into an old computer—nothing happens or it crashes. When you engage the body, mind, and emotions through creativity, the entire system spontaneously upgrades. Students are naturally eager and enthusiastic about sharing their creative skills and insights. They enjoy teaching their peers, it gives them self-esteem, a sense of purpose and value.

I also feel that they've come to accept each other. In the beginning, some of the learners that we have in the Brown Paper Studio group would like to argue all the time. Now they become friendlier with each other, there's a camaraderie that they have with each other now, they'll stick up for each other. You can see that Brown Paper has actually broken that as well and they'll come pass and they'll hug each other. . .so the development of that especially has changed the learners. Now they'll intermingle, they'll speak, they will laugh at each other and they are not angry at each other. Yeah, the integration it truly happens.

Glendale Educator

Number two is that students actually want more responsibility for their world. They know they are thriving in a healthy culture, one they can introduce to the larger learning environment. It is the critical developmental stage for self-governance and engagement in civil society.

Yeah, they have grown tremendously. . .one grade 9 learner, was someone that wasn't as outspoken as he is now. He always used to be this strict jacket and he would sit quietly in class, up in the corner. . .I think he is the most outspoken person now. . .he's grown tremendously, he stands up for his fellow learners.

Glendale Educator

Number three, it is cheap, low tech, labor intensive, portable, and fun.

ALL of our learners have passed to the next grade in the Brown Paper Studio. ALL of them have a 100% pass rate. It gave them confidence—"I can do something."

Glendale Educator

A 100 percent pass rate speaks for itself. No one wants to listen. We write lots of grants to public- and private-sector funding sources. The public sector ignores us. The private sector gives minimal awards under tightly restricted guidelines to implement programs that are essentially for public relations purposes. These minor grants are decoration for end-of-the year giving reports that are about marketing and have little to do with real community development. We're in the non-profit rut of just enough funding to flounder.

Next to my son, Salim, Althea Trout, known far and wide as Tia, is my most faithful company member. Tia's been with me from the beginning and somehow she reminded me of myself. I didn't know why in the moment we met, yet our years together demonstrate that this self-contained young woman has the same grit and fire as I did at her age. She doesn't waste time with the word *impossible*. Using outdated computers and text messages on cell phones, Tia and I run Brown Paper from my little square office at UWC. We write cover letters and proposals, create budgets and schedules, organize transport and food and performances and tours. If I am six thousand miles away and she tells me something needs to happen, I trust her judgment. When I'm fresh off the plane with empty pockets, full only with ambitious ideas, she puts rand in my hand—some small stash from a grant tucked away in the corner of a cabinet, just enough to keep me going until our next ship comes in. As on the street, she and I know that "word is bond." Tia came to Brown Paper with an itty-bitty voice, now she easily commands any size room of children, teenagers, or adults. Her vocal presence reflects her sense of authority, autonomy, and womanhood. She is my right hand, my first officer, a natural-born executive. Without ever having to explain myself, she understands why I continue with this madness. She is my art daughter. After watching us operate together to produce *Looking for Mike*, Hanan testifies, "Mommy, Tia is your child."

Our challenge now is to open another Brown Paper Studio as theater-company-in-residence at Azaad Youth Services in District Six. We are invited by Azaad's executive directors to convene as part of an innovative project integrating job-preparedness training with creativity and life-skills development. There are already lots of programs in South

Africa that focus on life-skills training, typical talking-head workshops geared toward preparing unemployed or underemployed people to join the workforce. What makes Azaad's initiative different is the focus on creative expression. Although not formally a school, it is a learning environment of young people who were either underserved or rejected by the educational system. It's an opportunity to further document what I am discovering about Brown Paper Studio's efficacy in public education. It is the ideal next phase for Brown Paper Studio, except that we have no money to pay facilitators and we are already operating two studios, UWC and Glendale, on a South African shoestring. Our circle is being stretched to the breaking point.

Azaad Youth Services is in a perfect location on the lower slopes of Table Mountain, with views of the ocean and close to downtown and access to public transportation. It is housed in a huge, old, sturdy school building big enough to have a courtyard with palm trees in the center. Except for one other school and two churches, District Six was bulldozed to the ground, demolished during the heinous forced removals of the 1960s and '70s. The land is still mostly grass-covered vacant lots. In its heyday, District Six was a quintessentially Capetonian mix of people: Christians, Muslims, Jews, white, black, coloured, Asian, local, and foreigner. Known for a robust cultural life, District Six maintained restaurants, businesses, clubs, dance groups, and was the home of writers, poets, musicians, visual artists, an opera company and jazz bands. It was a magnetic crossroads where ethnicities mixed, made love and married, and therefore a threat to apartheid repression.

I sign a five-year contract for Brown Paper Studio's gorgeous, rent-free space in exchange for conducting workshops. We are collaborating with other artists, ceramicists, musicians, jewelry makers, photographers, recording artists, graphic designers, and clothing designers. We imagine a great union of creativity brought together to assist "previously disadvantaged" people find their voices and talents, while we as cultural activists build the community we ardently desire. It seems too good to be true.

The program participants, ages eighteen to twenty-six, are called *ambassadors*. Most have never stood up in front of a group to say their name, much less perform their own writing. Over the course of a year, we facilitate for 100 ambassadors. From that number, only one person does not make it to perform onstage. We work with groups of fifteen to twenty in five-week sessions. Every five-week cycle, we have to introduce the Basics, teach the games and exercises, devise an original script, and rehearse a new piece. All the ambassadors rotate between life-skills training, work crews, and the various other creative offerings. Brown Paper Studio is the most popular—when the new assignments are announced at the beginning of a new cycle, the group assigned to us cheers. They have already seen what their peers did and are eager to create their own show. The ambassadors come from Black and Coloured areas, and we excel at bringing together people who were conditioned to distrust and degrade each other. Azaad is a production pressure cooker that pushes us beyond our limits. We stretch. We hone our strengths as facilitators, dramaturgs, directors, and peacemakers. We got skills.

Despite the success of Brown Paper workshops, communication between our facilitators and the Azaad administrators is strained. They only pay for the cost of studio supplies, brown paper, and markers. We expect our studio to be renovated as promised, walls painted and floors sanded. We don't have a securely locked door and permanent space to store our equipment. As a compromise for our inconvenience, I negotiate for us to get transportation money. At least we don't need to pay to get to the building, since we all have to work elsewhere to make ends meet. Without our space intact and secured, we feel we are working for free. They feel they are meeting their side of the bargain by providing studio access. The coup de grace of our faltering relationship comes when one of Brown Paper's male facilitators becomes romantically involved with one of Azaad's female ambassadors. Regardless of the fact that they are both past age of consent, his behavior is inappropriate and sorely compromises our credibility. His official transgression is poor conduct while serving as a counselor at the annual theater camp; we all know it's really his amorous pursuits that get him busted. Over the phone I'm told by one of the directors that the facilitator in question can no longer enter the building. Regardless of his apparent guilt, I insist on a fair hearing for him. He is one of my most dedicated facilitators and has picked up the slack many times on numerous projects. I firmly believe everyone deserves to speak their side of the story.

We meet in the administrative office, seated at a big octagonal table, Azaad directors on one side, myself and Brown Paper facilitators on the other. It's a loaded courtroom setup. Before we begin, I ask if we can all move to different seats so that the room is not divided into opposing forces. We're supposed to be one program, one Circle, and no matter how we disagree, we need to position ourselves as such. Grudgingly, Azaad staff acquiesces. This repositioning results in all parties being able to listen and be heard, changing seats shifts the dynamic from those who are "in charge" to everyone having authority.

In the end, my faithful facilitator is still barred from the building, but without being disgraced. In the wake of the incident, any hope of collaboration is over.

By next year we are out. It was too good to be true.

My advocacy for public education comes from having been one of those considered "special".

My elementary/high school was private, prestigious, and predominantly white. Make no mistake, Dalton provided me with a first-rate education. It's just that I was one of the school's few Negro children, and it's not easy to be so young and so different. No doubt these early experiences influenced my decisions to attend public universities for undergraduate and graduate study.

Dalton had all kinds of resources: spacious classrooms, a big gymnasium, art rooms, dance studios, a large double-storied library, an elevator, a well-stocked cafeteria, and a swimming pool. Swimming was part of our physical education. Being overweight and pigeon-toed, I looked, at best, awkward in a bathing suit. On dreaded "swim day," I waddled into the pool wearing an old-fashioned white rubber swim cap, the kind with the button chinstrap. Everyone knows that when you go underwater, these dumb caps do not keep your head dry. My hair got wet. My hair had been chemically straightened, also called processed or "relaxed," a term suggesting that my hair normally suffers from free-floating anxiety. Every day for school my hair was bound into tight braids with the help of gooey, green Alberto 5 pomade. No matter what's been done to black hair, water provokes it back into its natural bush. The phys ed teachers were nice in a baffled, liberal sort of way, trying to lasso my enormous nappy braids into a rubber band. They were embarrassed and I was embarrassed. Finally one wrestled them into a sort of ponytail, something like an Afronytail. All the little white girls dried their hair and looked like they did before swim class. I looked like some wild hairy creature wearing those infamous sparkly blue glasses. I had to get into the elevator and go back to the classroom in this state. I had to face my classmates. People stared. I wanted a note from the nurse saying something about how my hair's emergency condition caused me to go home. Undoubtedly I became more alienated that day, looking like a freak in a third-grade classroom, feeling that, surely, there is something wrong with me.

Starting in sixth grade in Dalton, we were given homework assignments by the month. We learned how to plan, how to take a big task and divide it into small sections, how to prioritize. One of my strengths as an artist and director is organization. I approach chaos with a cool eye because at twelve years old I had to look ahead four weeks at a product. Too often I procrastinated and on the last possible Sunday night, wrote my reports, trusting my first mind to the writing. It wasn't a great habit. It also taught me that sometimes what happens at the last minute can be really good, and life in the theater is filled with the unexpected. It's part of the process, it's the wild card showing its face. It can be losing a cast member, publicity problems, technical snafus, personalities, panicking egos, financial shortfalls. You just breathe and look for the gift in the garbage. Crisis is truly an opportunity, and if you can trust that it comes for a good reason, you can find the good. In the final analysis, Dalton also gave me confidence, because despite the hierarchy of the world, I realized that being rich doesn't mean you're smart. Going to school with the upper class let me know they are just like everybody else.

By the time I got to high school, Black Power was evolving, and as an adolescent, it was everything I needed to know about who I was, since I obviously was not part of the Upper East Side. It was exhilarating to have something so radical to call my own. It was fine with me if I alienated my school friends—I was an angry Black girl and I only wanted to party uptown anyway. I knew every song on the R&B music charts. I was so grateful for WWRL, the Black AM radio station that played Motown and Stax Volt and all of the soul hits. After a long day pretending to fit in, I could listen to beats and lyrics that felt like me. I had albums by John Coltrane, Rahsaan Roland Kirk and the Modern Jazz Quartet. I sneaked into East Village music clubs with fake IDs. More than once music has saved my life. I did social studies reports on the Black Panthers' breakfast program and quoted Huey P. Newton in my essays. I went uptown to the Harlem YMCA barbershop and had the perm, the conk, the straightener taken out of my long "relaxed" hair. Once a reason for humiliation, ironically my big, bushy Angela Davis-sized Afro was now my source of pride.

I become aware of the field of Applied Theater in the locker room after a yoga class in New York while chatting with an actor about my work in Cape Town. "Oh wow!" she says. "So you're doing Applied Theater over there." *I am? Is that what it's called?* I think to myself. I go home and google "Applied Theater." Flashbulbs explode in my mind like a racetrack photo finish. Here are pages and pages about this growing profession dedicated to using theater in social transformation. Applied Theater is gaining momentum as an academic discipline. Master's programs are appearing in the States at the same time I am building my own version on the ground in South Africa.

The growth of Applied Theater is huge for both sides of the globe, both sides of the brain. In South Africa, social disassociation comes from lack. As artists and cultural activists, we are constantly in survival mode, we rarely have enough. We have to make do with scant resources, scrounging for brown paper, markers, and fruit. In the United States, social disassociation comes from having too much: headphones, cell phones, computers, the bombardment of media devices, all of which get in the way of healthy human interaction. People are too wired up to greet properly, to say, "How are you?" and actually hear the response. The consequences are the same everywhere; the need for real-time spaces to connect to self and to others.

Brown Paper Studio is a replicable system that addresses a major issue internationally: public education. Public education is the way to profoundly shift any society. I speak to public education specifically, because most private and charter schools routinely incorporate the arts into their curriculum, they know creativity provides the developmental edge. Children of the digital age are learning more quickly than ever, so quickly, in fact, that it will be possible to effect remarkable societal change in a decade. Nothing of a truly progressive nature will happen anywhere until we address the issue of educating our children. There will be no economy other than a slave economy, there will be no ecology other than a dying planet, and there will be no peace or security for anyone, no matter how much money you have, until we commit to the creative potential of youth. All this is obvious to anyone who has used the arts for community development. By 2020 we must be standing on new ground, and it is possible for all of us to have an impact through the education of our children. We have less than a decade to make good on the democratic promises of both the United States and South Africa.

"You have done a lot for each other…now it's time to let go."

"He's drifting like a balloon in the sky…."

"He has a very difficult energy around him…it's old family karma."

All the psychics, energy readers, fortune-tellers, and well-meaning intuitive friends shake their heads. At different times and in different places, they concur: this relationship is nowheresville. I acknowledge the accuracy of their perceptions and ignore their advice. Thank goodness soothsayers don't know everything. I will leave Medi and come back to him more times than I can recall. Sometimes I don't even know if we're together are not, so enmeshed are our lives.

When his number appears on my phone, I wonder, "What now, what crisis?" When my number appears on his phone, he wonders, "How lonely is she? How much reassurance does she need this time?" In our blatant codependency, we are both incredibly glad that the other exists, is still alive and relatively well on Earth.

Why can't I forget this person? Why am I holding on to him?

The fragile shelter of our relationship lets me know for the first time in a long time that I belong somewhere. I've been able to make a life on the Continent, a life that allows me to redefine myself in the States. Medi gave me Africa as Home.

It's not always difficult between us. Most times it's the pleasant hum of domesticity, both of us searching for our lives in South Africa, both of us finding home in each other. Our plain, everyday rituals of chopping vegetables for dinner, watching soccer games and rerun American movies, sitting on the sunporch watching the sunset, hanging laundry, laughing about the nosy neighbors, unpacking groceries, driving to and from the university, talking about Brown Paper Studio, about the team, about friends and family, about Cape Town and Africa. It is one of life's sublime pleasures to have your man come in the door at the end of the day while you are cooking or tending to something in the house and or just being there, and as he enters the ambiance of your environment, it is similar to the satisfaction you both experience as he enters your body. He has escaped the pressure of the outside world for the sanctuary of you.

When my ninety-year-old mother and her dear friend Aunt Muriel visit for three weeks in October, Medi, just as he has done with Salim and then with Hanan, makes my family his family. He appears every morning, bright and welcoming, ready to take the senior ladies on their excursions to Table Mountain or to the township or to the botanical gardens for lunch. He is the ideal African host, protective, considerate, and patient with these elder women. He charms them with funny stories about clever baboons or about the time he was shipwrecked off the coast of Madagascar. When Mommy and Aunt Muriel depart Cape Town, he shows up at the airport, his arms full of cheap Chinese souvenirs to take back to the States. These trinkets are all he can afford, and even though the garish colored clock and plastic kiddie globe are from Taiwan, they are authentic African hospitality.

This is the year Medi and I have a soccer team, African United. He is the coach and captain. Our footballers are primarily displaced nationals from all over Africa who practice daily in the spirit of professionals. For their dedication they are paid only a few coins for transport money, on good days a couple of oranges. When we win, they get a beer. Sometimes they don't even have a practice pitch and play in the dust. We manage to save enough for proper uniforms and official equipment, and to celebrate World Refugee Day, we are invited to play Santos FC, one of Cape Town's two professional-league teams. We organize the event as the Unity Cup—complete with a trophy. To almost everyone's surprise, it is a true match. Within two minutes of kickoff, you could see the Santos players take notice, decide to really play, and shift their game into high gear. In the stands, refugee fans from all over southern Africa are screaming for our underdog team of dust and oranges to win this symbolic battle. The score was close, we lost four to three, and as in many close games, a questionable offside call drew heated debate. A sweat-drenched, beaming Medi is elated and undeterred. "It's okay, they cannot let us win, a little team from nothing cannot beat a premier league division team. We showed them we are professionals. Now they know who we are." He easily shrugs off the politics, savoring only the satisfaction of what his little team has done.

After our Unity Cup success, African United gains a reputation for having strong, disciplined players. We merge with a third-division team, Chelsea United, becoming unique in Cape Town for our diversity. We have Black South Africans, Coloured South Africans, Congolese, Tanzanians, Cameroonians, Rwandans, and Nigerians all playing together under the new name, Chelsea African. We physically embody the Unity Cup.

For the first half of the season, we build momentum, doing well and moving up the third-division table. Then, without warning, Medi's partner sells Chelsea African's license. He is a working man, a South African living in Mitchell's Plain. The enterprise of running a soccer team has exhausted his funds, and he accepts an offer without consulting Medi. We have no legal recourse. We foolishly operated as an informal alliance, postponing a written contract until the second half of the season with the thought that we'd be in a stronger position to negotiate once we ranked in the division. All the work, over a year of time and the investment of hard-earned money: gone. We aren't even told who owns the license. Disheartened, Medi's players disperse, leaving him with nothing.

The devastating sale happens while I'm in the States, my return delayed once again while I raise funds to travel. Medi calls me in shock. In every phone call, he repeats the same phrase over and over, the way traumatized people speak. "It's gone, my team is gone. It's gone, what do I do? Tell me, what do I do?" I blame myself. Why wasn't I more business minded? I'm as stupid and gullible as he is to believe in people. It's the story of our lives to be ripped off for what we do best. Although I've never believed in luck, I'm starting to think that I am dealing with someone who is fundamentally unlucky. Misfortune follows him like a cloud, and I get rained on all the time.

A few weeks later when I fly into Cape Town, I don't call Medi to pick me up at the airport. I ask Miki to come get me, and I stay with Ingrid until the tenants who are subletting my flat vacate. I want to see him and I don't want to see him, and it seems that my heart has lived on both sides of these tracks for years now. I'm prolonging my own misery. Medi thinks somebody is going to save him, discover him, "Bring him up", as men like to say. Some agent, some employer, some boss man will recognize his worth and make it all better. It's his colonial indoctrination, his version of the same sad dogma of suffering and salvation that still enslaves most of the world. There's nothing I can do about it other than disown my similar, deluded beliefs. More than once in Cape Town, I will pin my hopes on someone recognizing Brown Paper Studio's value and coming to our rescue. I, too, am hooked on the savior myth.

At Ingrid's big lovely house out near the ocean in Muizenberg, I walk alone by the water for days, gathering courage to tell him I'm back and that we are through. Finally, I call.

"Allo."

"Hi."

"Hi! Where are you?" He sees my voice has popped up on his phone as a local number.

"I'm here in Cape Town, out at Ingrid's."

"Oh…When did you get here?"

"A few days ago."

"Why you didn't call me to fetch you?"

"I didn't want you to pick me up. I didn't want us to see each other."

"Oh…Where are you now?"

"I told you, I'm at Ingh's."

He cuts straight past my defenses. "I will come to see you."

"I told you it's hard for me to see you, it's too difficult to be together. It's too much."

"I will come there."

"Please don't."

I don't mean it. I want to see him. I want to have everything be all right and him not be a refugee and always broke, making his way in the world with his clothes held together on the inside with duct tape. The same questions echo: why do I still care, why can't I let go? Because when I call, even as he is in the midst of some new despair, and I ask, "How are you? How is your spirit?" he says, "I am good. I have me. I have myself." He didn't read it in a self-help book or hear it at a motivational seminar or find it on the Internet. He knows it and teaches it and lives it. He is it. "I have myself."

After my "Please don't," he stays silent on the other end, waiting for me to soften, to slowly push the creaky door to my heart open and beckon him back in, the one who has the key to the lock.

Finally he says, "I'll call you tomorrow" and of course I concede. He hears the tumblers click into place. The next day we walk on the beach; it is foggy and cool, much like our communication. Despite the tension we are relieved to be in each other's presence, caught in a chemical reaction that is stronger than reason. We sleep on the single-person cot in Ingrid's guest room, make the love we've both been longing for. Our bodies are spoons, our breathing is deep. Just as we have always done, he kisses the back of my shoulder and I kiss the palm of his hand, our way of saying goodnight.

For years I will consistently sabotage these moments, some of the happiest days of my life. For a long time, I didn't believe I could have what I dearly wanted: his commitment, his companionship, his comfort. It was right there all along. Where there is no trust, there is no true intimacy. Medi and I are our own circle, going round and round on a track that has no destination.

I resist calling Medi my man, introducing him always as "my friend"—after all isn't my man supposed to have credit cards that work and an official title? My man is supposed to show the world who he is so they can know who I am. Medi does not submit to my superficiality; despite being near penniless, not once does he let me snub him for his lack.

One day I am fixing myself an avocado sandwich and wondering why, despite my devotion, I always have one foot out the door. Standing at the kitchen counter, I am jolted by the real reason. The thought renders me motionless, and for long moments I just stare at the thin, lightly salted, green-gold slices lined up neatly on buttered toast the way Medi has always prepared for me. Underneath all the stress and strain of having to constantly support him financially is an even worse shame. It is the molten core of my insecurity about this conflicted love affair. I can buy him clothes, cars, and things galore. Ultimately it is not what I can give him that shatters my confidence, it is what I can never give him. I cannot have a baby. I am too old. I cannot make him a father, and African men are expected to be fathers. It is a duty and an obligation to their family, a source of pride and joy for themselves. The fear that he will leave me for the mother of a child haunts me. I never allow myself to be totally at ease. I never exhale.

𝄢

2007

Breath
Cancer

All true benefits are mutual.

Elisabeth Kübler-Ross

"**G**irl...did you fill out that application?"

Liz's voice goes up at the end of her sentence in that slightly accusing way sisters sound when they're about to get on you about something. I know what she's going to ask—if I have submitted the application to Semester at Sea, a liberal-arts program that has been taking faculty and undergraduate students around the world on a ship twice a year for over thirty years.

"Girl, I'm so busy just holding down Brown Paper, balancing two worlds six thousand miles apart, I don't know if I can afford the time."

"You can't afford not to, now just do what I'm telling you to do. Fill out the application and send it in."

Liz was the communications professor on the fall Semester at Sea voyage three years ago. Since then she's been on my case to apply. Liz is a tall, red bone woman with dreads down her back. She moves in the unhurried way of folks used to walking down country roads, although don't let her sensual stroll fool you, she's a stone city girl from Compton, California. She's also a formidable scholar and a prestigious artist. We met at the Fulbright orientation conference in Washington, DC. I was on my way to South Africa. She was headed for Zimbabwe. We bonded instantly.

One reason I'm a good director is I know how to follow directions. I submit my application in July and don't give it a second thought until nine months later, when an e-mail pops up from a professor by the name of Mike Maniates asking me if I want to sail around the world teaching theater. What's a Girl to do? She gotta go.

Traveling means I must leave Brown Paper in the capable hands of Tia and Salim while I gallivant across the globe. They will rise to the occasion. Hanan will accompany me, as she has applied and been accepted into the program, the hitch being that her home university refuses to transfer her financial aid award to Semester at Sea. The night before we are scheduled to depart for Nassau to embark the ship, I get a phone call demanding I make arrangements to pay her tuition or she will not be allowed to board. I am as determined as a mama bear that she will go with me, and I sign over most of my check. I'm damn near working for free.

Semester at Sea is advertised as the "voyage of a lifetime," and it is the opportunity of a lifetime. It ain't no picnic either. The shipboard community is made up of undergraduates going very far away from home, most of whom don't know each other until they arrive onboard. The faculty is professors from a variety of universities and colleges who must leave at least some of their academic ego at the door, behave nicely, and quickly form a teaching cohort. All of this happens while encountering thirteen totally new countries and cultures and living on a vessel that never stops rocking.

It's a trip for real.

Arriving in Bahia

It's five a.m. and I'm wide awake and excited about arriving in Salvador de Bahia in Brazil tomorrow morning. We have one more day of classes before we are in port, and will be there for five days during carnival. It's dark still and I can see the lights off the north coast. I savor the comfort of the ship and beauty of seeing the sky and the ocean every day. I hold my office hours just before lunch out on the deck, that way I can relax and read or plan my class sessions and I'm first in line for food. I have my priorities.

It's said that the Amazon is the lungs of the earth, and I suspect it's true because Brazil is surely the heart of the planet. Brazil wins everyone's affection, and the fact that we dock in the middle of a world-famous carnival makes the love affair that much more passionate. We spend four days in a place where the music, bodies, dance, food, skin, smiles, and color are ablaze in high definition ecstasy.

"Taking a picture is like taking anything, you have to ask permission first."

We're crossing the Atlantic Ocean from Salvador, Brazil, headed to Cape Town, South Africa. I'm the only teacher of the arts and the only Black faculty member. I'm addressing the student body in our daily global-studies class, referring to their habit of intrusively snapping pictures on slick cameras and high-priced cell phones in the impoverished sections of the countries we are visiting. They mindlessly click shot after shot as though the world we are sailing around was designed for their enter-tainment and subsequent posting on Facebook. I've noticed that most Americans, regardless of age, race, or gender, only consider themselves to be having an experience if they can eat it, buy it, or photograph it. Otherwise, they have no way to enter into the moment. Consumption equals reality.

"See people before you photograph. Connect to them," I advise. "Acknowledge their presence. Whenever possible ask permission to photograph their faces, their children, their homes. You are looking into their lives. You are taking something and it's not for free. The price you must pay is to pay attention."

To their credit, the students are actually hearing me. The room pays attention. Later several students will quote me as we travel. On our many field trips, I notice an increased sensitivity, a moment of pause and respect for the incredible diversity of life and living we are privileged to see.

The young woman who boards the ship with me in Nassau, Bahamas, is not the same person who disembarks in San Diego; Hanan sheds one skin and grows another. Through sight and smell and touch and taste, she learns that as humans we are indelibly more alike than different. She discovers her mother in a distinct way, witnessing the effect I have on my students and colleagues. Hanan and I drop anchor in the Bahamas, Puerto Rico, Brazil, South Africa, Mauritius, India, Malaysia, Vietnam into Cambodia, Hong Kong, People's Republic of China, Japan, and Hawaii. Together we party at carnival in Bahia and reunite with Brown Paper Studio in Cape Town. We are seduced by the cultural collage of Penang, silenced by the atrocity of the Killing Fields, enthralled by the splendor of Angkor Wat, enchanted by the gracious precision of Japan. Crossing the waters, we are born again as mother and daughter, emerging new from the same salty womb.

For our port stay in South Africa, I organize a field trip called Brown Paper Studio International, taking a busload of students and faculty to visit the Cape Town Brown Paper Studio sites. We are still operating at Azaad in District Six, and along with a tour of the building, the American students see evidence of the country's tragic history of forced removals. At Glendale, our proudly South African teenagers take the college students firmly by the hand and lead them through a Brown Paper Studio session. My shipboard students later comment that they had never seen such confident high school youth. We complete our day at the University of the Western Cape, where Brown Paper Studio facilitators introduce their peers to our home studio. My company has prepared poetry and performances to welcome us. As a guest lecturer, Miki eloquently recounts the history of UWC's activism against apartheid. Filmmaker John Fredericks discusses his acclaimed documentary, *Mr. Devious*, about the legendary Hip Hop artist from Cape Town. John's impassioned talk dovetails perfectly with the fieldwork assignment for my shipboard Brown Paper Studio class. One of my students' course requirements is to document in their journals the presence or absence of Hip Hop culture around the world. I want them to notice clothes, language, movement, gesture, visual media, and, of course, music. Without exception, every country we visited has evidence of Hip Hop—they are becoming aware of Black music's potent cultural impact around the globe. Before we leave UWC's campus, South African Brown Paper and Semester at Sea Brown Paper are all talking intensely, engaged in small animated groups, exchanging contact information. These are the connections that reshape the world.

Glorious Cape Town

Brown Paper Studio International went brilliantly. On the bus home, all the Semester at Sea students were crashed out sleeping. It made me laugh because South African students have to be very tough to work hard for many hours at school and jobs, plus traveling long distances in public transport. Once they get home, they have to actually cook their meals rather than order takeout. Today was a very special day; even my toughest critic, Hanan, is impressed.

On the ship my cabin is informally Black Women Central. We Sisters literally keep each other afloat in an environment where most of the people of color are crew, primarily men from the Caribbean and the Philippines performing the invisible jobs of cleaning cabins, bussing the dining room, cooking, and janitorial maintenance without any days off. We know all these workers by name, we make a point to acknowledge their excellent service. To maintain some semblance of sanity, the Sisters and I gather under the radar in my unusually large, comfortable cabin. My only emphatic request prior to boarding the ship was for a bathtub. Wherever I am, I consider my bathtub to be my second office, listening intently to the messages I get while submerged. I sent an e-mail to the program administrators explaining that I teach with a lot of movement, and decompressing in a tub of hot water is a requirement at the end of my long day. As a result I was given accommodations big enough for a married couple, plus with a private balcony. On a vessel filled to capacity, space is a premium and my space was luxurious.

When we dock in Cape Town, I manage to smuggle a full case of wine into my cabin, the official limit being two bottles of alcohol per port. When the pressure of being the Other gets overwhelming, as it often does, members of The Sisterhood— Dia Draper, Shayla Griffin, and Sherri Barnes—gather in my room to drink, tell jokes, and tell the truth in our own rhythms. The masks we wear as Black people are sometimes so imperceptible we don't know they're on until we've taken them off. Although I meet some outstanding colleagues and many memorable students, it is still generally misunderstood that in the best of interracial company, the constant reality of being perceived as a minority is a full-time job. I say *perceived* as a minority because, American institutionalized racism notwithstanding, most of the world is in fact people of color. Having to scrupulously maintain clear boundaries about who you are and who you are not requires a Sisterhood.

Dia is the program registrar and one of the sharpest administrators I have ever known. As the saying goes, Dia "knows no strangers." She has a laser-beam mind, matching wit, and can bring a room to order with a glance. On more than one occasion, Dia's spiritual and material largesse saves my and my daughter's day.

Sherri is the assistant librarian, a woman who has made her practice of library science into activism. She easily provides resources and context for the social and political issues we encounter as travelers. Sherri and I take public transportation and walking tours to inexpensive places off the beaten path in the countries we visit. We are economical adventurers.

Shayla is the program's administrative assistant and the unofficial guardian angel of the voyage. If we ever need to negotiate with local people for goods and services, we send Shayla in as our ambassador. People melt in her presence and wonder what they were so upset about in the first place. In our most expensive port, Kobe, Japan, I check my bank balance online and read the notice that the IRS has garnisheed half my savings for back taxes. I started the voyage in deficit, now my only nest egg is cracked. I'm in shock. It is Shayla's embrace that steadies me when I feel like giving up.

Hanan and I are definitely on the discount tour. Due to our budget constraints, I bring back bottles of hot sauce as souvenirs from every country. I manage to purchase a few modest gifts for friends and family and treat myself to one extravagant treasure, a custom-made ring of imperial topaz from Brazil. I watch my colleagues buy artwork and wardrobes, enjoy fine dining at restaurants, take leisurely side trips. Compared with many of our shipmates, Hanan and I are broke; but in the majority of countries we visit, we are considered rich, a perspective that make us appreciate everything even more.

India Update

Greetings from India! We're due to depart tonight and set sail for Malaysia. Everyone says "India changes you." You think you know a little something about Life, and India smacks you upside your head with incredible majesty and unyielding poverty side by side. The proximity of the sublime and squalor is overwhelming. You must submit to both. You are changed.

Our shipboard community is incredibly fortunate to have Archbishop Desmond Tutu as the Distinguished Lecturer for the entire voyage. On my daughter's twenty-third birthday, I ask the Archbishop if he would kindly stop in to her surprise party following one of our People of Color @ Sea meetings scheduled after every port visit. These gatherings are a way to process our external and internal journeys as students, staff, and faculty of color and the more we see of the world, the more we experience a sense of unity. I arrange for an ice cream cake with candles to suddenly appear toward the end of the meeting. The Archbishop arrives right on cue to hug a deeply honored Hanan. At the end of the one hundred days at sea, our executive and academic deans comment that this was their most peaceful voyage ever. I attribute that in great measure to the guiding presence of the Archbishop, whose absolute authority regarding self-respect and mutual respect permeates our shipboard community.

Although I did not overeat on the ship, I found myself slightly overweight for the entire voyage. Once I got home, the bloating disappeared, the extra padding really an emotional buffer expressed as body fat. Trapped in a rolling vessel, all the conflicting and revelatory feelings of hundreds of personalities are amplified by the fact that you are surrounded by water. Seasickness and homesickness are rampant. Everyone is going through an evolution. We are a collection of different people, visiting different countries, teaching and studying different disciplines. It is hardly a glamorous trip. It is definitely not a cruise. It is some of the most demanding teaching I have ever done, and I have taught in some hard-core spaces. It is worth every moment.

Moon over Penang

A full moon wanes somewhere in Scorpio, and I've had marvelous day. The visit to the drug rehabilitation center, then shopping with Hanan and friends, then she and I have a long dinner at Kapitan's 24, my Penang café hangout. It's rush hour and the streets are lively and the restaurant is busy in waves. We eat masala chicken, cabbage, garlic nan,

roti, rice, dahl, and pineapple and mango lassi. She smokes cigarettes and we talk about
everything, Bollywood videos are on the screen, and middle-eastern funk is the music.

The children across the street in the Muslim shop play for the hours as we sit. The
little boy takes off his clothes and runs around the street naked for a while. The night lights
come on, and as we leave the restaurant, we hear the evening call to prayer. Rich incense
rolls from the shops with the flamboyant gold and jewel-toned saris of little India. On
the other side of the street, the Chinese businesses are closed and silent for the night. The
whole world is riding a motorcycle.

Hanan tells me she notices it is different to be a woman here in a Muslim country.
There's little chance of being harassed or leered at, although here, as everywhere else in the
world, she effortlessly commands the attention of men. I could sit and talk at that sidewalk
café for hours each day simply feeling the pace of people, their desires and carelessness, their
kindness, and their fragility—each person a whole story.

"Mommy, Grandma Lee Anna died."

Hanan and I are in Cambodia, undoubtedly our most intense field
trip of the voyage, when she gets an e-mail with the news of her grandmother's passing. How is this possible? How can we be so far from home
when we lose our beloved Ma? We are sitting in a sumptuous hotel suite
in Phnom Phen staring at each other in shock. For the next three days, I
am the trip leader, responsible for sixty people, and it's not until we are
back in Ho Chi Minh City that we can call our family in Louisville.

It's close to midnight when Hanan and I get back to Vietnam. We
find the makeshift Internet café that doubles as a garage, the place full
of students and local people. Over the sound system, Mariah Carey sings

about being a hero. Hanan is crying with her father on the phone, saying how much they love each other, how much they love Ma. Shahid reminds Hanan of how proud her grandmother was of her scrappy little grand-daughter. They are mirror images of rebelliousness. Hanan has Ma's graceful, articulate feet and hands. They could be each other's teenage portraits. I get on the phone to Shahid, mostly listening as he gropes for words to wrap around his grief. At this crossroads in life, there is not much anyone can say, only the language of the heart is big enough.

I can feel Ma's peaceful presence; she has prepared herself as best as possible to cross over. My brother-in-law Stewart was Ma's young-est son. He died two years earlier. Alternately, he lived the fast life of the streets and the slow grind of prison. Both mother and son died of cancer. Both were resilient, resourceful, indomitable spirits. Stewart made everyone laugh, especially at themselves, and Ma loved to laugh as much as anyone I have ever known. By nature she was a true medicine woman, her home a safe haven for family, friends, and stray souls. The angels wish they could eat real food just to taste her cooking. In the temples of China and Japan, I light incense for the ancestors and I speak to Ma. As slender smoke curls up to her seat in heaven, I thank her for teaching me so much about how to raise babies, how to make the world's best chili, how to be forgiving and fierce, and how to know when each is appropriate. Across Asia I honor my mother-in-law's earth journey, telling her, "Now you're everywhere Ma, you're with us all the time."

Beauty and Horror

We sail through polluted seas in Asia. We approach Vietnam. I am close to tears when, in one of our global studies lectures, I see the proud red flag with its bold yellow star and remember how we felt about this tiny, valiant, undefeatable country. "No Vietnamese ever called me nigger," and with that phrase, an alliance was formed with the entire colonized world that had ever suffocated under the boot of white supremacy. We were never the same after the sight of the My Lai massacre on our televisions.

The big trip of Hanan's and my voyage was three days in Cambodia. I impulsively selected this excursion mostly because I was fascinated by Angkor Wat, a stunning complex of temples built by Khmer royalty. The other part of the trip was to the Killing Fields, a site of horrific genocide under the Khmer Rouge in the late 1970s. We stand before the massive glass shrine filled with human skulls. We are there on an auspicious day. It is the annual offering of prayers and flowers by local monks to release the souls who were tortured to death on this ground. The holy men chant continuously as we walk among mass graves. Our three-day visit was a mind-altering combination of awe-inspiring beauty and shocking images of evil. Brazil and Cambodia have been my most unforgettable ports, their impact indelible.

The entire shipboard has gathered in the auditorium to hear the Archbishop's final talk of the voyage. He opens his lecture with enthusiastic praise: "Did you all see the Brown Paper Bag performance last night? Fantastic! So professional! I want to nominate them for an Emmy." The misnomer doesn't faze me, as Brown Paper Studio has been called Brown Paper Bag more than a few times. I'm flattered big-time, and I know the Archbishop means that he wants to nominate us for a Tony, one of the most prestigious awards in American theater. Everyone is buzzing from our spectacular opening. We had a full house and a standing ovation. As the audience was leaving, I heard people saying they were going to come back tomorrow to see the show for a second time. The next night we are sold out, standing room only. I've forged my Brown Paper Studio class into a performing ensemble to create our own original production in a matter of weeks. Because there are twelve official ports on the voyage, I name our show *The 13th Port*. The 13th Port is the Heart.

The show is structured as old school Hip Hop battle with a male and a female actor as two MCs and the rest of the company cast into competing crews. Because our show opens the night we cross the international dateline and since we all live that strange repetition of the same calendar day, our script begins with the classic Twilight Zone line "Imagine, if you will,..."

The 13th Port has taken the ship by surprise. Maybe the most surprised are the cast members themselves, who aside from opening-night jitters have no idea how a showcase of this kind—the standard Brown Paper method of sampling everyone's writing with improvisation, movement, and plenty of popular dance music—is going to fly. They are overnight sensations. Their friends see them differently, the performers see themselves differently. As I was told once, "Thank you for giving me the dream I never knew I had."

One young actor was particularly uneasy before the show. In his self-doubt, he was spreading dissent within the cast. "It won't work... we can't do it...this show's a mess...we'll look stupid." I recognize these nerves. I am brave in the face of such fears because I have some version of them myself on every show. Each time they arise, I must focus harder, get clearer, affirm deeper. It's actually a major part of any creative process to push past what you think you cannot do. In our postpartum discussion, he raises his hand. He looks me full in the eyes and in front of the entire class says, "Judyie, I want to say that I'm sorry. I didn't realize we were going to do what we did. It was great." To his immense credit, he didn't address me privately off to the side or send an e-mail. He declared his apology publicly. Brown Paper was a place for us all to not know, to catch each other, to grow.

Another young male actor wrote about being in love with a man. I doubt he believed I would include his delicate confession as part of the script. I am almost sure he had never uttered such a statement in public. In rehearsal he always ran over the lines, mumbling them quickly. I was patient. I knew that this truth about his sexuality would create a safer space for us all. I coached him. "We need your voice. Let us hear you." At the opening, his voice rang like a bell. His honesty was a booster rocket for the entire company to stretch their boundaries. Everyone got louder.

I Love Japan

As anticipated, I am in love with Japan. We're in Kobe, a small port city that has marvelous fashion, food, and ambiance. It's also mad expensive. Japanese people are very friendly. If you ask directions, they will walk you to where you want to go. The city is busy and surprisingly quiet. People don't talk much on the streets and don't raise their voices. I can't imagine what they think when they arrive in New York and encounter Black people out on the corner talkin' loud. I guess they fall in love with us.

Dia and I spent a spring Saturday afternoon just walking around, enjoying the sights. The clothing shops are fabulous and the Japanese people stay sharp. There was a lovely park in the center of the city filled with blooming azaleas. We browsed a couple of wonderful Hip Hop and R&B music stores where the owners took pictures with us. The day before, I went on a field trip to an awe-inspiring Buddhist temple, the largest wooden structure in the world. The temple grounds were teeming with Japanese schoolchildren, all wearing bright yellow hats to match the budding forsythia.

We set sail tomorrow for Honolulu and then arrive in San Diego in two short weeks. We'll cross the Pacific and the Ring of Fire. We'll sail through our fourth full moon. Dear Family, we'll be glad to hug and kiss you all.

When Liz meets us at the dock in San Diego, I am totally spent.

I am dumb.

Without so much as a hello, I fall into her arms sobbing.

I have been around the world.

I am humbled and exalted.

I am different in ways I can't yet possibly understand.

Months ago, as I prepared to travel around the world, I decided it was over for Medi and me. Before I sail on Semester at Sea, I resolve not to call or contact him. At all. Ever again. This makes sense to my fevered brain until we dock in Cape Town. After twenty-four hours, I instinctively dial his number. No answer. I hang up the pay phone with a sigh of relief. This is a good sign. We are done. Finally. Surely circumnavigating the globe is an ideal way to break up with someone. I continue my travels, confident I'm sailing away into a new chapter.

Back in New York after the "voyage of a lifetime" is over, I'm confronted with the reality of some major family issues. My ninety-year-old mother has confused her accounts and allowed the rent to go unpaid for two months. I must find the money or face an eviction notice. The building has a nasty rental agent whose sneer when dealing with me is infuriating. After over forty years of our family's perfect record of paying the rent on time, I leave the office insulted and frankly worried.

I have no income in South Africa, a family to support, and a theater company to run. I am living on fumes. I stand on Eighth Avenue and Fifty-Fifth Street sobbing in the pouring summer rain, wondering how we will survive.

It's raining so hard, no one can see me crying or that the red dye on my soaked clogs has stained my feet like pale blood. I want to talk to Medi. His is the only voice in the world that can soothe me. His tone is the only sound in the cosmos that will do. I buy a phone card and dial his number.

"Allo."

"Hi. Medi?"

"Hi?"

"It's me. It's Judyie."

A pause of disbelief, hesitation, and then an exuberant "Hi!" and then "Hi!" again.

"How are you?"

"I'm okay. I'm okay. How are you?"

"I'm okay. I just wanted to hear your voice."

"Me too, I'm okay. I'm glad to hear you."

"Are you surprised?"

"I am surprised. You are quiet so long."

"Is this a good time to talk?"

"It's good. It's fine. How are you?"

We fumble along like this for a few more sentences. It is less about the words than the feeling pulsing through the phone line plugged directly into our hearts. I can see him in his shadowy, solitary room, the habitual late-night TV glowing blue, his meager belongings organized neatly on the floor next to his mattress.

We continue our stuttering, coded conversation. Before I know what I am asking, the words tumble out, "Did you pray for God to bring me back?"

This time there is no hesitation in his voice. "Yes," he says, "yes, I did."

"Your homework is to breathe. Sounds easy right? Observe yourself over the next few days. Notice how many times, you are holding your breath. Notice how often you are cutting off your own free, abundant Life Force. Push the reset button. Breathe."

This is always my first assignment in training actors because it is the most essential aspect of inhabiting a human body. I tell every student that if all you learn to do in my studio is to breathe, you have learned everything. Sounds simple? It's a lifetime proposition. To truly understand the teachings, one has to breathe. Breath makes space to integrate knowledge. Breath is our connection with source, respiration is to "re-spirit," the aim of "in-spiration" is to invite spirit. I know how crucial breath is because mine was held hostage. At the age of thirty-eight, I was diagnosed with Hodgkin's lymphoma stage 4B, the most advanced progression of the disease before you die. I had to restore the use of my left lung after it collapsed under the pressure of a rapidly growing tumor. Metaphorically I had to learn to breathe for myself, to put my need for oxygen first, just the way you are instructed on airplanes.

You never forget the day you were diagnosed with cancer, it becomes a marker for your mortality. "Your disease is very treatable," the doctors tell me, sounding almost hopeful. What they dare not tell me is how painful the treatments will be. I remember days when my hands hurt so much, I could barely write. I did write. Words that let me know I was alive inside a jagged shell called my body, tender, distended, swollen, inflamed. Sleep was more like a collapse into paralysis, something beached and breathing heavily. My journals reveal sentences like this:

I hurt. I drink water. I pee. I urinate. I am here. I am here. I hurt.

Clumsy mantras to blow on the faint embers of me. My children terrified and courageous, some dim recollection that our souls had promised to go through this. There was no other reason to live. Marriage. What? Career? Whatever. Death seemed if not easy then at least possible, compared with the prospect of living in a dead paradigm. Staying alive was for the benefit of those two small, sweet, trusting people who seemed to love me for no other reason than I was their mother. I was enough as their mother. That was me. That much I knew.

I hurt. I drink water. I am here. I want to sleep.

I want to sleep and wake up again even if I do hurt, because they will be there, sometimes watching me close, making sure I inhale and exhale.

One hideously painful morning, my son walks into the bathroom before dawn. I open and close my eyes in a mute pulse. Blinking hurts. His baby feet are bare on the white tile. His favorite Mickey Mouse pajamas are high-waters, faded to a dimly smiley Mickey because he won't let us throw these old treasures out. He sleepwalks in, sees me on the toilet in some altered state of pharmaceutical haze and pain contractions. He smiles his movie-star smile. He pats my knee. Cheerful.

"Okay, Mommy. Here you are. I thought you had to go to the hospital again."

He rubs his face and turns to walk out, satisfied I will not die. I will live another day in these busted aching pieces. I will be his mommy for as long as he needs me to be.

After my physical recovery from cancer, I attend a Life, Death, Transition workshop at the Elisabeth Kübler-Ross Center in Virginia. During a horoscope reading, an astrologer perceptively describes my illness as "the door to the cage"—if day after day you have to affirm why you want to live, you begin to believe that your life is more than a set of obligations to other people. Being alive is not about death and taxes. Life is to be cherished. I arrive at the remote EKR facility in pitiful shape. I am like a doll that has been pulled apart and had her arms and legs screwed on wrong. I am doubtful this arduous trip into the mountains of Virginia is all that necessary. My therapist, Ruth, who works as a facilitator for these intensive five-day residential workshops, practically insisted that I go.

"Why Ruth?" I protest. "I've been to lots of therapeutic, spiritual, and creative workshops. I know my progress is good."

"One week there is like spending a year with me."

For her to make such a claim is significant. I heed her wise-woman's advice.

In Elisabeth's groundbreaking process called Externalization, the expert staff conducts an orientation by leading a group of anywhere from twenty to sixty people through a series of discussions and processes, including singing and drawing with crayons. These casual, disarming activities steadily bring us into an increasingly open, available state.

We're being prepared for "mat work," the core of Externalization, where participants and facilitators sit on the floor in a large open space, outfitted with a single bed-sized mattress that is "the mat," piles of phone books, boxes of tissues, pillows, towels, and short pieces of rubber hose. One by one, of our own volition, we come to the mat to release the pent-up, congested, paralyzing pain that has deranged our bodies and spirits. Howling and screaming and crying and shaking, we pry open the places where we are so stuck we can no longer function. It's these atrophied places where our diseases of the body and mind fester. Digging up these tangled roots is strenuous. We're as frayed and fitful as we have been since childhood. People weep, vomit, go into regressed states, as they push past the locked doors of themselves. What happens on the mat is true catharsis.

How can people be so naked? I cannot believe it. *No way*, I promise myself. *I'm not going up there and revealing what no one knows about me in front of complete strangers.* Hour after hour I sit entranced as participants cleanse themselves of the debris of shame. By the end of the second day, during an evening session, I start to get restless. Agitated by spirit, I cannot sit still. Unannounced, my guardian angels swoop in, pick me up, and walk me to the mat. It is not a conscious decision, and it is one of the most lucid moments I've ever had. I can no longer resist the urge to see who I am underneath my threatened ego.

I sit on the fresh sheet that is changed after every person "works." I look into the eyes of the facilitator and instantly break down crying. I pick up a piece of rubber hose and indicate I am ready to smash the phone book to pulp. Despite months of physical therapy, my arms are still weak from cancer treatment. Clutching the hose, they slam down again and again as the thick yellow books shred under my fury. The layers of defense that led me to this moment begin to unravel. "Be a good girl." "Be a good drone." "Be a good nigger" "Be a good... —the programming of decades starts to collapse. Torn paper is flying everywhere. My frail arms are mighty.

"Say what you need to say, tell them how you feel," the facilitator urges me on as I unleash the pathological niceness, the ruthless conditioning to fit, to conform to a dead system that never has and never will accept me as I am. I pound phone books until I slump over. Who knows what I say in my ranting. I go into an altered state where my beleaguered body starts to wake up. My cells hear my wailing. "At last," they say, "she wants to live." The facilitator asks me to look out at the faces of the other participants. I'd probably just thrown the worst tantrum times ten in my entire life. I look into every single face, and what I see there is total acceptance, compassion, understanding. I had no idea acting out could feel so good.

I was done for now. I come back to subsequent workshops to continue my self-restoration. Somewhere in the process, I decide I want to be on the other side of the mat. I want to facilitate. I am a theater artist with no training as a social worker or nurse or psychologist.

One of the Center's directors answers my request:

"It's not about degrees," she says, "it's about the heart. If you make it through the training, you can facilitate."

In my intensive training, I learn about the body and the psyche in ways that profoundly inform my theater practice. Externalization facilitation training helps me read energy. When you are sitting next to the mat, all of you must be focused on the individual doing his or her work. Your ego must patiently sit in the corner and wait for you to come back. When I facilitate mat work, I even visualize a small version of myself in a chair in the corner watching. The amount of energy required to be present with another person is massive. The amount of energy needed to stay present with your self is even more. That is the level of self-awareness I expect in Brown Paper Studio.

Elisabeth Kübler-Ross was a pioneer of the worldwide hospice movement. Her seminal book, *On Death and Dying*, brought the process of death out of the shadows of the American psyche. Although I was trained in Externalization by her senior staff, she continued to lecture and answer questions on the last day of our residential workshops. Confidentiality is a cornerstone of Externalization. From Elisabeth I learned that if you betray confidence, there is a strange reciprocity that will cause your careless indiscretion to be revealed. It will come back to haunt you. Sound spooky? That's exactly the word Elisabeth used for spirit guides. "People's spooks," she called them, those invisible beings and energies that look out for us from our first breath up until our last. When a person finds the courage to speak out loud the abuse that they suffered or the abuse they inflicted, when that person is ready to release the burden of shame, it is a sacred act. To indulge in gossip or sensational storytelling is a disgrace, and you will sooner rather than later be busted by the universe. Elisabeth was an iconoclast. She never bit her tongue. She pushed you to be authentic. In her later years, she could be found casually smoking cigarettes outside the facility's kitchen or inside making cherry pies for the workshop participants. "All true benefits are mutual" has become a principle for my life and for Brown Paper Studio.

Journal Entry, New York

This is not a near-death story,

this was the edge of staying alive

ravaged by the disease

ravaged by the treatment

pounds of flesh melting away, waking up swamped by your own sweat

breathless to the point of suffocation

surgery, chemotherapy, radiation

needles pierce your lower back for bone marrow samples

implants under your skin like a Star Trek borg

burning your hair off with radiation

poisoned with seven chemicals so toxic you need three more drugs for the side effects

eyes so sensitive you have to wear dark goggles over sunglasses

throat so raw you can't swallow, only suck ice cream through a straw

taste blindness means nothing has any flavor, you could be eating the newspaper or mashed potatoes and not know the difference

nausea only incessant weed smoking relieves, then you get the munchies

but you're too sick to eat

you inject a refrigerated drug into your stomach and thighs

you learn to shoot up, an official junkie.

The Dreaded Prednisone lets you sleep for only three hours at a time

withdrawal is violent stomach cramps, paranoia, hallucinations, nightmares

imagine standing in the shower for five minutes not knowing what to do,

what's the procedure for taking a shower?

crying because you're asked by your mother to make a salad

you don't know what she means

you can only stare at the lettuce in tears

gaining heaps of weight, fat and bloated and pale and hairless

constipation on top of constipation

a digestive track of cement

having to go to the emergency room to have the crap blasted out of you

losing hair first on your vagina

speechless in the hospital shower seeing clumps of your hair

suddenly clog the drain

vomiting with nothing left to vomit

the pain of shingles buckles your knees on the street

sends you straight to the pavement

the doctors give you a prescription for Delaude, the surefire pharmaceutical heroin

one hundred pills' worth 'cause they know you're gonna hurt so much you'll use them all

and you'll be back for a refill

you barely recognize your own limp arms covered in sores

you lift them wondering "where do these belong?"

Maya Angelou read a poem at Bill Clinton's inauguration

your only vague recollection of three whole weeks of your life

when you're tattooed for radiation they tell you those marks will never come off

for your whole life however long that may be

you'll always have the map, the coordinates where they shot radiation into your lungs

technicians scurry out of the room, slam the solid lead door behind them

leave you lying on a metal table thinking

"this is what Frankenstein felt like"

you laugh a lot

some of the shit is so ridiculous you feel like you're watching it from far away

maybe you are

watching it from the future

a future where you are tanned and glowing and healthy and loved and hiking up a

mountain with the same lungs they said would never function again

you laugh because you are a phoenix

It is late July when I leave New York and finally make it back to Cape Town. Glendale Brown Paper Studio is now a company of eighteen members who have been together for two years. They are eager to write their own play, and our facilitators began the creative process weeks before my return by asking: "What is the most pressing issue in your lives?" Their answer was not AIDS, not gangs, not drugs. Their answer was hatred between people of color. Deciding on this topic was in itself emotional; I was told students argued and cried, discussing the hostility between Black South Africans and Coloured South Africans. By the time I arrive, the company has come to consensus that the biggest issue they face is the chokehold legacy of apartheid. It is destroying their education and threatens to destroy their future. Glendale Brown Paper describes classrooms that are divided down the middle along "racial" lines, to cross one of those lines is to risk your reputation and sometimes safety. They are subjected to favoritism from teachers raised in the crippling system of apartheid who knowingly or unknowingly perpetuate their prejudices on those "Born Free," the name given to the generation born since South Africa became a democratic nation. Blatantly and subliminally the "Born Free" inherited the madness of apartheid. On our first day at Glendale, we discovered young people who had been in class together since they started school and had never spoken a word to each other across that invisible barrier. Our nascent, hopeful community in a crumbling system wants to tell the world it is possible.

Using our standard techniques of collective writing, improvisation, movement, choral language, short scenes, simple costumes, and a basic set, we devise a half-hour piece, *Just a Name*. When I enter the process as director, the script is already well-developed, and in September we plan to premiere the show at Glendale during a special school assembly. The vicious words said behind Black and Coloured doors will be onstage. The principal knows what a volatile topic we chose. He fears a violent reaction, he also knows it is too late to shut us down. The word is out about our show.

The audience loves it. "Gervaalik!" they shout, Afrikaans for "Dangerous!" Coming from adolescents, this is quite a compliment, because it means in the eyes of the youth, we have challenged the status quo. We are speaking the unspoken. We are daring to turn the light on. In the postshow discussion, our actors share the process of creating the play and speak eloquently with their peers about why they chose such a taboo topic.

We present *Just a Name* to the Department of Education administrators as a way to propose a tour of the school district. In contrast to our student audience, the performance is met with stunned silence. The agency's director stands and commends the cast. Then he asks, "Is it really like this?" The company looks at each other. Is he seriously asking this question? Does he not now know how dire the situation is in the classroom? Does he ever go and visit the schools? That level of either ignorance or denial baffles the actors, for a moment they say nothing.

"This drama program has given me a way to be seen and a way to be heard," ventures one actor, a young Black woman who will matric in a few months. "Before Brown Paper Studio, I could not come to you and speak this way. We are telling you the truth about how it is for us every day."

The agency director applauds the importance of the message; he concludes that the show must tour the entire regional district as a way to promote cooperation and understanding. He pledges his support for our production and requests a proposal to expand Brown Paper Studio to other schools in the district. As we are leaving, a secretary pulls me aside. "I want you to know I don't use that kind of language." Her whispered disclaimer indicates that maybe a lot of other people do. After numerous calls to the Department of Education, a meeting is scheduled where we finally submit our proposal. We never receive a response.

In December, at the end of this exhausting year, I leave for the holidays, the festive season, as it is called in South Africa. Soon Medi will make his way to the Congo. He has not seen his mother in seven years, and at some subconscious level, he already smells the fires of xenophobia that will sweep South Africa within six months. News media will publicize the most graphic display of this violent madness: the image of a Somali man being burned alive, collared in a flaming, gasoline-soaked tire because he is "kwere, kwere," a foreigner, an outsider accused of stealing jobs and women. Chronic deprivation within the masses of South Africans breeds pockets of reactionary fury directed at displaced people, who in many cases have already been driven from their homeland by war. Medi intuits that things will only get worse for him if he stays in Cape Town, and the primal need to see one's mother calls him home to DRC. What he does not know is that home will not be a respite—it is its own furnace.

When I arrived in Cape Town in November 2003, it was too late at night for Medi to get public transport to my apartment in the chic northern suburb. We had to wait until morning to meet on the street across from the beach. We had not seen each other since our February affair. Coming upstairs we were spellbound, amazed that each other was real. He picked me up and carried me to the bedroom.

"Did you miss me?" The question all women ask all the time.

"Yes."

"How much?"

He pointed out the window to the water. "As deep as the ocean."

I believed him.

I still do.

Today is the last time I will see Medi for a long time. The airport is strangely quiet and empty, as if it knows we are sad. We have been through a lot together. He has been robbed, cheated, burglarized, assaulted, hospitalized, humiliated, locked up, lied to, even rejected by me with his bags packed by the door, and welcomed home again.

So much defeat.

There is a big patch of sun on the terminal floor, and as the time drains between us, the rectangle of light grows dim and disappears. There is nothing to say. We hold hands. Why did we waste precious moments with old beefs, useless quarrels?

The announcement is made that my flight is departing. We press close together, letting the truth of our shoulders and cheeks replace words. Once through the security gate, I send a text message: *I love you. Always.*

Little words on a screen smaller than a matchbook.

Do I really understand there is no way to know if our shoulders and cheeks will ever be close together again?

Part Three
Water Damage

2008

Eye Contact
Sex

Journal Entry, Cape Town.
I wonder if they can see my scars.

Life is hectic. I am doing too much. Maximum output, minuscule input. Underfunded projects held together with chicken wire and spit. I am too many places at once, teaching the ABCs with no XYZ backup. No replenishment, no nurturing, no lovemaking, only booty-call sex. After all this time, I'm back to square one.

There's a scene in the movie *Training Day* when Denzel Washington taunts Ethan Hawke about having sex with his new wife. "I'll bet you still fuck her face-to-face." For a few beats, we, the audience, are deer in the headlights, realizing what being eye to eye in bed means—it means you're making love. We calculate how much face-to-face fucking we've been doing, and the absence of eye contact means something is definitely missing.

Eye contact is "I" contact. Not limited to physical sight, eye contact is literal and metaphoric. As a Brown Paper Studio basic, it is about allowing another to see all of you. Eye contact is fully available to the visually impaired, since the real requirement is being comfortable and confident with oneself. There are many ways of perceiving: with fingertips and touch, hearing and sound, definitely through silence. We could all learn a great deal about how to see from people who are blind.

You cannot make theater without honoring sex because you cannot dig deep into any true motivation without mining the body. A director must identify the sexual energy in the script, whether subtle or blatant - it is always there and will come up in the studio to be used as creative force. It's volatile and has to be harnessed for the stage. All of the stories, all of the dramas are eventually about sex, because our fascination, fear and obsession with sex is linked to our core creativity.

Brown Paper Studio enters Glendale's show *Just a Name* into Artscape's High School Drama Festival. Many of the province's secondary schools with formal theater programs compete in this major annual contest. The first round is at the Zolani Cultural Centre in Nyanga Township. For the past two weeks, South Africa has experienced widespread outbreaks of xenophobic attacks, and while we are performing inside, outside police in riot gear chase looters from the shops of Somalian refugees. Helicopters circle overhead. Shots are fired. All the festival participants have to be barricaded inside Zolani until the disturbance is contained. *Just a Name* features a scene about xenophobia where two township girls deride their girlfriend for saying she would even think of dating an "outsider." Our script is on point. Out of forty-three entrants, we are among the thirteen finalists selected.

Just a Name is an unconventional piece for a teen drama festival, a penetrating look at the effects of internalized racism. Our non-linear script of all original student writing is a style of experimental theatre that sets us apart. We are the largest and most diverse cast in the competition, our eighteen Black and Coloured Glendale actors remain onstage throughout the performance. We use physical theater techniques, simple costume pieces over T-shirts, chairs become all the scenery, props are minimal. The dance is fresh, choreographed to the latest music. We exude marvelous ensemble energy. The *Romeo and Juliet* theme of a Coloured man in love with a Black woman is provocative. By the middle of the show, our high school audience is on their feet, shouting back at the actors, cheering at the dance section, a reaction reminiscent of our first show, *D'CIPHER*, years ago at UWC. We are definitely the people's choice.

At the awards ceremony, *Just a Name* is completely ignored. Our actors cannot believe they get no mention, not even a nomination, not Best Ensemble, not Best Original Show, not Best Script. Nothing. I urge the actors to address the judges at the reception—after all this is an educational event and they have invited the students' questions. One adjudicator dismisses *Just a Name* as "not universal enough." The students are criticized for presenting the problems of South African racism between Black and Coloured people out of context. One of the judge's retorts: "If they were going to touch on such a sensitive political topic, why didn't they talk about the history of apartheid?" The message from the officials is obvious: "Do not raise issues adults cannot deal with."

"Sometimes the greatest indicator that your work has hit a nerve is when no one wants to recognize it—at least not yet," I tell my young actors. "In a few years theaters will be looking for a piece as honest as *Just a Name* and you know that you were way ahead of the game." Initially bewildered at being snubbed, by the end of the afternoon, something magical occurs. It is the alchemy that happens when people go through the fire of performance together, when they have to depend on each other under the pressure of stage lights. The youth decide to trust their experience; they have become their own authority. They know they did a fine job and that they made a statement. "Gervaalik!" indeed. By the time we leave Artscape, Glendale Brown Paper Studio is walking arm in arm in the late afternoon sun, singing the South African national anthem, "N'kosi Sikelel' iAfrika." They are the most exquisite rainbow nation one could imagine.

Free for All: Meditations on Democracy is Brown Paper's last production at UWC. We are working in a hostile environment, the Centre does not want us there, the sentiment that has been insinuated since the beginning has become overt.

To keep pushing myself creatively as a director, I stage *Free for All* in the round, on a square stage that has the feel of a sports arena. We are able to devise a good script in short order. For the first time, I challenge myself to include sections of the performance that are wholly improvised. The audience enters into the chaotic theater space where chairs and props and costumes are thrown all around, the actors are onstage, frozen in aggressive poses as if in a brawl. Their breathing slowly becomes audible and animates them into bringing order to the space. Gesture and sound organically create language, and characters start to appear. Costumes are our all-purpose, ubiquitous T-shirts painted by the actors with words describing various random and perhaps contra-dictory identities: sexual, racial, class, ethnic, economic. At the show's climax, everyone turns their shirts inside out to reveal the word "Free." *Free for All* has fine writing and a willing ensemble. What we don't have is support. Wearily we make it to our opening in UWC's Ithuba Arts Festival. My cast is happy. That's a blessing. I, on the other hand, am getting burnt out.

At the same time I am mounting *Free for All,* I am teaching my most difficult Memory & Vision class, a small group of talented graduate students who never quite form a cohort. I am at wit's end at being shut-tled from room to room at the Centre for the Arts, lose my patience, and blow up in anger while giving notes on the students' first-draft scripts. I didn't realize how upset I sounded until our feedback session. Thank goodness for feedback sessions where you have to hear about yourself. I listen and I am humbled and know I can't teach or direct at UWC again anytime soon without compromising my standards. I am not being valued because I am not valuing myself. What will it take for me to say, "Enough"?

From the studio window, I watch Tia walk down the road to the taxi stand at the school gate. She walks slowly, her back to the Centre like she never wants to see it again. She has a plastic bag in her hand, some few things she gathered from the office, a paltry package for someone who has given so much, so wholeheartedly. She's looking at the sky or the trees with an aimless relief at having finally made a decision to move on from a situation that was only proving more pointless. Tia is leaving Brown Paper Studio. I miss her already. She quit. I don't blame her one bit. Who in their right mind would stick around after the money you raised was incorrectly allocated essentially draining your budget, you must raise the money again and still manage your program that is gasping for air? Me, that's who, holding on for as long as I could. I ought to run down the road, too, if I have any damn sense.

Tia lost her partner two months before, missed being by his side at the hospital on the morning he died because Glendale Brown Paper had a show at the Department of Education. As her man, her mentor, her lover was taking his last breath, she was driving costumes or props or some such thing down the highway to perform for a bunch of people who couldn't care less. She missed holding his hand and whispering her final "I love you" for a sham, for people who had no intention of fulfilling their commitment to us. As I watch her amble away, angry and out of my life for what I hope will not be forever, I know a chapter has closed. Tia was Brown Paper Studio's backbone. I will have to depend even more on my son to keep us alive. Our company is growing and disintegrating at the same time.

On the edge of District Six is a big old building that was once the Sachs Futeran department store. It has three floors of loft spaces with broad wood-planked floors and wide windows facing the city and the harbor and the mountain. It is right in the central business district, walking distance from the train and taxi stations, and across the street from a friendly bar with great pub food. Everyone can get to us. The collaboration between Brown Paper Studio and a company of independent management consultants occupies the entire top floor. Our marriage of business and art audaciously sets out to ignite Cape Town with an unprecedented vision of creativity and commerce. Our space on Harrington Street becomes a lively, humming laboratory.

The business consultancy was founded by a farsighted, independent woman from Cape Town, who relocated to the more cosmopolitan environment of Johannesburg to pursue her passion for facilitating transparency and accountability in the public sector. Her partner, the Cape Town office director, along with one of his associates, visited Brown Paper Studio during our yearlong residency at Azaad. Impressed with what they saw, they invited us to bring Brown Paper Studio's process to the business world.

Our first project began the previous year at the Clothing Industry Bargaining Council of the Western Cape. It is the administrative arm of one of the largest unions in the Western Cape and handles medical, dental, retirement coverage, and contract disputes for a union of more than thirty thousand workers. We were contracted to do a two-hour workshop for midlevel managers. Before we left the building that afternoon, we had created such a buzz, we were invited to come back and conduct workshops for the entire staff of 137 over a series of three weeks. Our follow-up sessions received positive response. Now in 2008, our next phase is to create an original performance addressing the most pressing values issues at the agency. Based on a survey circulated in all departments, the key values identified were respect, service delivery, teamwork, and trust.

From the Clothing Industry Bargaining Council staff, a dedicated core of twelve people volunteer to devise an original piece, *Trust on Tour.* Except for singers in church choirs, our small ensemble is new to performance. They are male, female, black, white, coloured; coworkers who take a giant step toward new relationships with themselves and each other over the weeks we work together. They are each other's best cheerleaders.

A makeshift stage has been erected at our Harrington Street loft space, where we mount two performances to accommodate the entire agency's staff. More than half the employees climb the three flights to see what this performance is all about. They are surprised, most pleasantly and a few uncomfortably, at the show's candor. *Trust on Tour* causes something of an uproar—what happens now that what was said only in private is public? When you ask tough questions, unpopular sentiments will be raised getting to the answers. People are not robots; you cannot use art and creativity to reprogram them to be content in unacceptable circumstances. If they choose to express themselves, they will wake up. Theater asks them to pretend to be other people who are just other parts of themselves. Their subdued self will emerge and throw a fit if you tell it to shut up and sit back down in the office cubicle again. They will resist. Brown Paper Studio is not designed to make the machine work better.

Do businesses really want significant change? Do corporations really want transformation; new relationships that will threaten the status quo? Probably not - they want more productivity, more compliant employees, so as artists we get caught in a space of doing feel-good, fun-time recreation sessions.

The system relies on everyone behaving themselves and not feeling too deeply about anything, including, and maybe especially, their role in the system. It's how control is maintained, keeping people separate from themselves and then from each other. Making a sound and unlocking bodies become subversive acts. How many times did I come back into a workplace and was greeted heartily with, "Here comes the lady who makes sounds! Are we going to move around and play games?" After an interactive session, the meetings where you sit and are talked to by PowerPoint slides become intolerable. Brown Paper Studio is more than cosmetic.

Management wants us and at the same time they don't. It's the issue I faced at UWC, where it was okay for students to participate in the Centre for the Performing Arts, just don't get them riled up. Art is supposed to rile you up.

What Brown Paper Studio does is deeper than a stress reliever or an ice breaker or the entertainment before a corporate lunch date. It requires time and a willingness to change. It demands risk. It is an intentional transformational space, meaning you come in knowing you're going to come out different, and the difference is not what you planned or expected. That difference is your growing edge. It happens to me every time.

The use of the Internet café in DRC is too expensive for Medi and me to communicate. We exchange one e-mail all year:

Dearest Medi Santos,

I miss you and wonder what's happening.

Cape Town is a very lonely place without you, Salim is generally out with friends, at varsity, training, etc. I'm alone too much, no one to hold me or talk to me or sleep with me or make love to me. In some ways I want to leave South Africa because of these feelings. Although I enjoy my work, I know there's more to life than just working. You know how I love to cook and be close and listen to music and watch movies. One has to feel cared for and appreciated by someone that makes their heart smile and sing. Loving and being loved, that's what is most important to me now.

My life is taking a new direction.

Please tell me, what are your plans to return? I don't know what is happening with us. We have to find a way to communicate. Is there any way for you to be at a land line or at least send me an e-mail? I hope to hear from you soon.

I Love You,

Judyie Ella

These long bouts of celibacy are a big no-fucking drag. I indulge in what I call a misdemeanor, a casually intense/intensely casual affair with a younger man who appreciates a grown woman with a healthy appetite who is pretty much always willing and able and does not want to marry him. Such trysts start out fun and end up heartbreaking, because once activated by carnal desire, women have a tendency to fall in love and lie about it. We play ourselves cheap, acting like we don't care and wishing he would call more often. We unfurl like a stubborn flower that doesn't have any more sense than to bloom over and over again, even in the cold. I want to tell the countless women who love like me that it's not our fault we love so hard. We didn't do anything wrong.

Hi

How ru doing ?it was so nice to hear from u. hope u r doing well. im doing well, to go to kinshasa i will need some money that why im steel here. i will be back soon im than with my passport. for now things r hectic im looking foward to come back. my Judyie just be patient u will see me soon. i love as much i can not leave u. my training is fine with one team i m training with. i love u Judyie keep ur hope,i m with u in spirit day nite.

take care love u so much.

With love

Medi Santos

Pun intended, the best sex is yet to come for everybody because our bodies and spirits are upgrading to something new, to a divine human, a highly evolved harmonic of flesh and joy. Notice how much better sex is when you feel good about you. The path is self-appreciation and I know what all the self-help books say: "You've got to love yourself first". I do. I promise. I also love skin against skin and heat and the undeniable smell and sound of desire. So I sell out time and time again. I wonder if they can see my scars?

Way back when, during my first Fulbright year, Medi lived with me and Salim for a few weeks. One evening I answer the door, and Medi is standing with his arms outstretched, holding a puppy.

"Who is this?"

It's a small, shaggy mutt, some kind of Yorkshire terrier yard-dog mix, a female, very sweet. She is wiggling to get down.

"This is Pookie." He places Pookie on the floor, and she skips in like we are old friends, sniffing around with approval at her new digs.

"What? Are you serious? You got a dog?"

"Yeah, I buy her from the man near where I used to live." Medi has a matter-of-fact tone and strides in after the dog. He's looking at her with pride. "She is nice, neh?" he says grinning the famous grin. "She is my dog."

I have a thousand thoughts. Where is this dog gonna live? I mean, she's cute and all, but Medi is just staying with Salim and me temporarily. Who's gonna walk this dog? Who's gonna buy her food?

Pookie has made herself comfortable on the couch, contentedly licking her paws. Medi steps outside momentarily and returns with a couple of cans of dog food, a dish, a leash, and a collar. I wonder, is this dog even house trained? A dog is a big responsibility. A dog needs stability. I have not been considered. This is all too much, blah blah blah blah…I reach my boiling point.

"You must be kidding! What made you decide to get a dog?"

"Ach, Judyie." Medi turns his palms up in exasperation. He sits down next to Pookie on the couch, shaking his head and looking at me as though I've asked the world's most obvious question. Then, in his infinite patience, he lets me know: "For the feeling."

My middle name is Ella, given to me by my mother in honor of vocalist supreme, Ella Fitzgerald. Every morning I awaken with one thought: *I want to see my mother.* This trip to South Africa is the longest time she and I have been separated. Somewhere in the middle of this eternal winter of 2008, I decide to start using "Ella." I hope being a namesake has sufficient mojo to catalyze my life upward, or at least get me home for a visit. Before I open my eyes, before I am conscious, before I stop dreaming: *I want to see my mother.* The longing for her nurturing presence makes my body ache.

One night, I just lose it. I'm too high, too tired, too frazzled, too lonely. I'm scribbling page after page in my journal with my nondominant hand, praying my subconscious will give me some clues. By the time the sun comes up, I've managed to hallucinate that yesterday evening I carelessly gave away a rare and valuable coin to the taxi driver, and if I can reclaim it, I will collect a fortune and be able to retire. All freaked-out and half-dressed in my nightclothes, I run out into the street to stop the same taxi driver and ask if he has my magic five-rand coin from last night. My hair is standing up on top of my head, my breath is bad from smoking, my eyes are red from drinking and swollen from crying. He looks at me like I'm insane, curses in Afrikaans, and speeds away with a van full of impatient morning commuters. Back in the house, I call Miki, who must hear the lunacy in my voice. Straightaway she comes over, takes me to her house, situates me on the couch, and feeds me. She indulges my babblings. I am too embarrassed to tell her about the coin episode. A few days later, I discover that my magic coin is, in fact, South Africa's newly issued five-rand currency appearing everywhere in the country.

Except for excursions to the theater with Miki, I'm spending too much time alone. Cape Town can be socially desolate. Without my sweetheart, I am sensually invisible. I have my new frolic, Mr. Misdemeanor;

unpredictably he calls, rough and ready, hoping to catch me home alone. After a couple shots of booze and a few tokes, he comes on strong, like the best espresso. He only takes off his boots and pants, leaving his socks and shirt on lest I get the silly notion that this arrangement has some sort of permanency. I hide his two cell phones in the other room—I am well aware that for this generation, nothing is sacred, and know how much they relish documenting their every move. I don't want to be a featured YouTube clip, carrying on with my behind up in the air. After the deed is done, more or less to all parties' satisfaction, he replaces his pants and boots, checks his cell phones, and makes a getaway in his sporty car. I have no illusions about having been just another pit stop for this brash young man who was gassed by banging Professor Jump Off in her stylish downtown apartment.

I drink wine alone, eat dinner alone, smoke a joint alone, and crash, hoping I don't wake up until morning. If I do wake up, the only way back to sleep is to get high again, and I am tired of playing with myself to ease the dry spells. I sink deeper and deeper into isolation and fantasy. In the ebb and flow of the moon's phases across my barren bedroom floor, I concoct an erotic escape, a surrealist sex landscape starring Everyman, where I can ride the high tide of my desire...

Crescent Moon

we are in a hotel room
filled with roses
we have nowhere to go nothing to do
only love each other talk touch bathe sip water massage
you are over me I rub my hands over your body your chest your nipples
arms face buttocks

I kiss you everywhere
I smile at you I say I love you
over and over
we move slowly gently there is such peace in our togetherness
sometimes we are rough and wild and you enter me from behind
I'm on my knees in the bed we cannot get enough of each other
we both refuse to come because we'd have to sleep close our eyes
not be able to see the other's face eyes
I dream of your eyes
how I can rest in your soul for hours
the roses are smiling they are honored to witness such love
such lovemaking
they gladly blossom and pulse a scent
strong to match ours
I want to wash you I run a bath with lavender and sea salt
your skin is warm I kneel next to the tub
scrub your skin with the cloth
we are both crying
we are in a hotel room
no one knows us
we have nowhere to go

Half Moon

we are in a hotel room
outside a city moves restless broken resurrected
a city of Easter lilies and concrete breath
you are sleeping I get to watch you I get to stare I get to remember

the thousands of days I thought of you imagining ecstasy

this is ecstasy

this is without words

this is every poem of love of praise of redemption

this is new

no one could have told us how to do this

the universe wanted us to succeed prayed for us wanted us to kiss

kiss again so deeply everyone breaks into applause

because they are free too

we don't need to eat we drink champagne from each other's fingers

maybe suck a strawberry or mango

something sweet and light

to clear the palate for more kissing

I ask you to sing

sing anything

a nursery rhyme a spiritual a TV commercial

I just want the tone of your voice to wash over my belly

fill my vulva my ears the palms of my hands

so I can receive more love and sing along

without any tune

in our hotel room

Full Moon

we are in a hotel room

we are afraid of clocks that remind us we are going to die and have to

end this embrace

someday

not today

today we can still lie like spoons your hands on my breasts

you nestled hard between my thighs

was there ever any other place to be?

I walk across the room you adore me

sit on the end of the bed your hands on my hips

lick me from my throat to my knees and then again and again until I

stand there

come wet trembling into your mouth

I kneel with all the strength I have left

place my lips on the head of your altar and pray

not that old time religion not for anything we can't have not to be

spared damnation

or to fly to heaven 'cause like the song says

"this must be heaven"

I pray and answer my own prayer

my lips are divine

are god goddess alpha and omega

I take you whole in my mouth

receive you

you cannot believe Earth is not a dream

that this is all there ever was

we refuse to look at a clock

defying all the laws of gravity making time run backwards

or at least stand still

I lay back spread out on the carpet so wide you can see my heart beat

all invitation

you move to your knees

we freeze

we could come right now even

before the hard hunger of you pushes past the soft wet surprise of me

before you slowly hear the clocks grind to a stop

before you anchor your long thick darkness past my eager sugar skin tissue

so slow

oozing electricity

from the center of the planet through my lower back

time begins again

you are in

inside

your weight rests on mine our cheeks connect gentle

oh

you say

I cannot understand any language I'm busy inventing it

I place my arms around you

oh

I echo

we have discovered its meaning

it means that no matter what has ever happened or will ever happen

we are

We Are

we have finally discovered

Now

This is Now

no one ever has to regret anything for all of human history

everything is forgiven

you start deep penetrating circles

a rhythm that makes the roses blush

makes the flat champagne bubble again

makes the weary city take heart

its broken places glimmer and gleam light

oh

I won't say "I love you" because the words themselves have to end and
there is no end for

the love I have for you

a throb begins in my thighs I am lifted higher and I fall and before I
hit the ground

I am lifted again and fall again over and over I come up and slip caught
and carried higher

your tears run down my shoulder

your hands hold either side of my head

which is the only way I know we are not dead

the clocks break all around us shatter silently

everywhere everyone human remembers they are Divine

Oh Baby

I manage to translate the codes from the Earth's core

whisper in your ear

I can't tell where your tears end and mine begin

on the floor of our hotel room

New Moon

"nothing is ever over" you remind me

"every snowflake that ever fell anywhere is different unique one of a kind"

there was a time I wouldn't tell you I believed you

Now

I know you are right

about the snowflakes

there is a door in our hotel room

it will open one day and someone will come in

or we will have to go out

face the clocks the concrete the dead roses

the rhythm of our hips in the carpet will be a memory

it must be time to laugh tell a joke about mortality and passion

time to order a fresh bottle of champagne

to open the hotel room door

feel the sea crash in turn over the chairs tables submerge the bed

flood out the windows I don't care

I learned my lesson well I know what love is

you taught me well

while I was masquerading as you

there is no death only orgasm

they call it "the little death"

do they call death "the big orgasm"?

there is no rush

we can take a shower hold hands let steam melt our bodies

I can never lose you

I've taken you so deep we broke the time barrier and

I can always hear you sing because

I'm no longer afraid of my voice

Just as suddenly as Pookie enters our lives, she is gone. A few months after we adopt her, I get in the car and she is not there. Medi has moved into a rooming house and picks me up every morning to take me to the university.

"Where's Pookie?"

Medi shrugs, expressionless. He gazes straight ahead at nothing through the windshield. "The people in that house they complain, they say she cries all day for me. They say she makes too much noise. I must move her out. I take her back to the man where she come from." He turns the key in the ignition and shifts the car in gear. "When I leave her there, I tell that man that she is my dog and that I will be back...I say to him, someday I will be back to fetch her."

2009

Trust
Theater

The world does not need saving, the world needs you to be you.

Out There!

If 2008 was a Bitch, 2009 was Her Mama.

It all crashes fast.

My bank account is on perpetual empty.

My mother's eyesight is failing.

My son flunks out, loses his university scholarship, and breaks ups with his girlfriend, all within seventy-two hours.

My man and I have not been together in over a year.

My hit-and-run Casanova gets religion and deserts me for Jesus.

...and it's only February.

Barack Hussein Obama is the forty-fourth president of the United States.

It might be time to Head West.

"What you are looking at is one of the most marvelous examples of Greek architecture, the theater at Epidaurus, built to honor the god of theater, Dionysus." It's the late 1990s, and I'm mesmerized, sitting in a University of Massachusetts graduate school seminar listening to my directing mentor, Dick Trousdell, lecture on the origins of Western drama. He passes around a large book of photographs. I study the picture and caption, reading that "to this day the splendid amphitheatre with its near perfect acoustics remains in use, large enough to hold fourteen thousand spectators, its graceful curves of limestone seats focused on a circular stage below." Across the ages, Dionysus speaks directly to my affinity for red wine and ecstatic experience. Dick continues teaching: "Epidaurus was built adjacent to the Asklepion, a healing center and sanctuary. People came from throughout the Greek empire to discover remedies in their dreams. Patients were brought out before daylight to watch comedies and tragedies performed as the sun rose on the hills behind the actors. Going to the theater was known to bring the mind, body, and psyche into alignment." I admire how Epidaurus is constructed in harmony with the earth, a round, feminine venue where we were able to watch our stories as the light dawns. At this critical juncture of the twenty-first-century paradigm shift, we need places to imagine and experience our wholeness. In contemporary theater, the lights go down before the show begins, we go into the dark, momentarily slip into the subconscious before invoking the magic of make-believe. To the ancient Greeks, theater was medicine, each visit a chance to make ourselves anew.

Theater is about openings and closings. I have left it more than once, and I have always come back. My professional career began at the

Public Theatre as an understudy in *Les Femmes Noires*, French for "The Black Women." The play is a spare, lyrical landscape of Black women workers in New York City, structured as short vignettes. Our large cast's image is captured in the classic photography book documenting Black theater, *In the Shadow of the Great White Way*. In one short scene, I played a young lesbian talking to her lover on a street corner; this was the early 1970s, and Black female same-sex relationships onstage were still a frontier. As was the practice at the Public Theatre, about ten days out from the first preview performance, the producer, Joseph Papp, came to look at the show and give notes to the director. *Les Femmes Noires'* director was Novella Nelson, a Black woman well-known as an actor and a vocalist. On the morning of the run-through, two actors were ill, and since the show was double-cast, a total of three roles were missing. I had to cover all three, running up and down backstage, quick-changing costumes, snatching wigs on and off, and I did it all. In fact, I did it all so well that later Joe spoke to me privately in the Public's cavernous marble lobby, complimenting me on my performance, saying, "You are welcome to come and work at this theater anytime." At nineteen years old I was offered my own role in an off-Broadway show with some of the great actors of New York.

Not long after, I found myself in a real-life situation similar to the scene in the 1980 film *Fame* where Irene Cara is humiliated under the pretense of an audition. After business hours in an abandoned casting office, a director ordered me to strip naked to see if I could "really go there." Too frightened to fight back behind locked doors I could not run away. Although never touched physically, I was raped emotionally. I retreated far from the city for three years, time enough to gain courage, nurse my wounds and step back out. I was quickly hired by Ntozake Shange to collaborate on two shows; the first was a dream, the second a disaster. Young and still foolish in my late twenties, I hijacked myself into a disastrous affair with a professional colleague. It destroyed my self-confidence as an actor and I did not act again, this time for eighteen years. As the saying goes, "I don't have the legs for the business," something akin to what a boxer must endure to stay in the ring. I have the talent and not the temperament for the commercial grind.

All performing artists have war stories, not all go into self-imposed exile as I did. It was not only shame that drove me underground, it was my longing to be a part of a theater community where performers are protected. I dared to dream a world where artists are safe. I taught myself to direct and to produce my own plays because I wanted to be independent. I found work as a director and was making a name for myself developing new plays by Black women until I got badly bruised by reviews. That production convinced me to enroll in graduate school as I was determined to improve my skills. Personal traumas have driven my artistic evolution. It's why I am fierce about safety and mutual respect in the making of theater. I was sure there had to be a better way, and I have devoted my professional life to finding it. I passed up opportunities for a different kind of career that might have meant fame and possibly fortune. I held fast to a vision of a creative life that is emotionally sustainable. It's why Trust is the bottom line in Brown Paper Studio. Trust begins with trust in the self. It's a hard-won truth. It's how I am still standing.

I used to cry at the openings of Spike Lee movies, not because I was moved by the stories, which I enjoy very much, I cried because I wanted to be in the movies. I knew the actors and knew I was good like them.

Great like them. I'd be sitting in my seat in the dark and I'd be watching two films, the one on the screen and the other in my head, where I was featured and dazzling. Mine were not bitter tears, they were tears of frustration. In the words of my mentor, "Going to the theater was known to bring the mind, body, and psyche into alignment." Working in the theater ought to do the same. The oracle part of me was sure my decisions would one day bear fruit. In spite of invisibility and ridicule, there would be a harvest. I had to be patient. The New Days would come.

Prospective corporate clients are coming to visit our attractive loft-style offices and studio in Cape Town, taking an interest in our "offerings," basically Brown Paper Studio workshops geared to the needs of business facilitated by myself and senior management partners. I feel like a prize poodle performing for stressed-out customers, getting them to buy into the arts as a way to boost productivity. Those business clients who participate have a fulfilling experience; still, the sales pitch is skewed. I am constantly being asked to prove that what we do is effective. I am so invested in having our collaboration be successful that I do not listen to my inner promptings that we are not quite speaking the same language. We are not yet on the same page. Having been around long enough to read the handwriting on the wall, I still ignore the warning messages. One of my company members says it best: "I feel kinda squeamish referring to ourselves as a product." As art and business partners, we need to take more time to define our common value system. There is no bottom line in art, no final reckoning of value, because those measurements cannot be applied to being human, and that is the purpose of making art, to encourage us to be more human.

I know I will become exhausted and ultimately ill if I continue to work at this pace of facilitation, constantly introducing new people to Brown Paper Studio so they can decide if they want to sign a contract. "But you're the only one who can really do it" is management's response. If that's the case, then "it" does not exist, Brown Paper Studio is not real—it's just me and my specialized gifts as a teacher. I suspect that's not accurate, that the process can be transmitted and replicated, and that is why I must begin to formally train people. My partners agree to sponsor an Intensive Training to prepare Brown Paper Studio facilitators.

I design the best curriculum I know: performance skills, creativity techniques, how to devise scripts, required readings, practice facilitation sessions, yoga, improvisation, journaling, seminar presentations. It is a tightly compressed course equivalent to at least one year's graduate school study. We are a prototype group for what I project will ultimately be a state-certified, accredited training for Creativity Facilitators in South Africa. Any businesses we work with will be at the forefront. Art is crucial to the successful future of public education which is, in fact, the basis of any national economy.

Before the intensive starts the Cape Town office director discloses to me that I am being paid considerably less than what a male thirtysomething computer programmer earns per month working in our company. Apparently we are using the almighty capitalist standard for compensation, a system that values this young man's left-brain, quantifiable, linear skills above mine—a consummate professional who brings innovation, expertise, experience, and abundant human resources. In all honesty, the market's influence is only part of the equation and perhaps not the most important. The real reason a junior technician can be paid twice as much as I am is because I agreed to it. I said "yes" to inadequate money. In some dank, musty cavern of my self-image, I still believe that "just enough" to live on is all right. Decades of being a starving artist had me so brainwashed, I could not ask for what I am worth.

No matter how conflicted I feel about the financial inequity, I stand by my decision—the show must go on. Having never made choices for money now is not the time to begin. The intensive launches as planned on a Monday night in February. I am thrilled to finally be working at a level beyond introducing the rudiments of performance. There's only one way I know how to teach, which is to be present 100 percent, and we start the course in high spirits. In the syllabus, I share my noble-sounding introduction to our intensive:

Brown Paper Studio Intensive is a four-month course designed to prepare participants to be creativity facilitators with particular focus on the needs of business clients. As an arts laboratory we are continuing to develop a replicable, sustainable product based in performing arts practice specifically for the corporate world. Integral to the product's success is building an ensemble of talent equipped to staff the sessions, an ensemble that models the values and ethics we promote. As a participant your ideas, questions, initiatives, and enthusiasm are important contributions to the success of this innovative program. Our big vision recognizes business as a key platform for social transformation.

I buy a new journal with a graphic of an orange hand on the cover and record my teachings as Orange Hand Notes. On the first page I write:

Greet participants warmly.

Support the affirmative energy in the room.
Say Yes.

Some of the sixteen facilitators-in-training I invite to the intensive have been in the trenches with me since the beginning, art soldiers who have hung in there through thick and exceedingly thin. At long last, without fanfare or unnecessary explanation, Tia returns, testimony that the door is always open. There are new faces from among the business consultants' associates, enthusiastic recruits who have a gut understanding of the work. We are almost an equal number of men and women. We are artists, students, businesspeople, social service professionals, administrators. We are Black, Coloured, Indian, White—another dedicated tribe of Whoever from Wherever.

Orange Hand Notes:
Observe how people enter the room, how they walk, talk, move.
Observe how they respond to the open empty space, to the brown paper on the walls, and to each other.
Observe the effects of the warm-up.
Facilitation requires self-awareness, breath and body integrated.
Observe yourself.
Fall in love with yourself.

Week One...
orientation: reviewing the syllabus, introducing warm-ups and games, the importance of maintaining a journal, and of course, the Brown Paper Basics. Each single week of the curriculum was easily a month of

concentrated study, in some cases a whole semester's worth. I required full attendance, promptness, preparedness, outside research, and sweat equity for the studio space. I had to trust that the years of groundwork at UWC, Glendale, and Azaad would support this complete immersion. I distilled how I got to where I am as an artist, teacher, and facilitator.

Orange Hand Notes:

Your tools are breath, plenty of water inside and outside, adequate rest and sleep, journaling, drawing, recording dreams, physical exercise, spending time in nature, breath again, and gratitude.

We are simultaneously scientists and channels for spirit.

Self-appreciation is our product, practice it for yourself.

Week Two...

we choose seminar assignments; teams of two facilitators will read a book, present the main ideas to the company, and lead a discussion. We practice tableaus, how to tell a story using the body without words. We practice dreamscapes with dreams from journals.

Orange Hand Notes:

The most important book you read is the one you write. Journals are how you track and map yourself. It's The Book of You, and what could be more important than that?

Journals are a treasure chest of dreams—the waking kind and the sleeping kind.

Keeping a notebook is a requirement for an artist. How else do you document your process of digesting the world? "Know what you are going to say," we are told in primary school composition class. How can you know what you are going to say? It's all tangled up with feelings and if you think about it too long it will escape like steam from your overheated head and what you have to say will never make it to the page. Just like in the first Memory & Vision class, I remind the facilitators to write, "I don't know what to write," over and over until you break through the paralysis and your unbridled self says, "Enough of this! I know exactly what I want to say, and it makes sense to me." You are sitting on a volcano. You are a bucking bronco. Halting the flow of your pen over paper or your fingers on the keyboard to edit your writing in its first draft is a physical habit. When physical habits are removed from the body, habits that keep you comfortable and believing you are safe from the passion of yourself, the volcano erupts and the horse throws the rider and you morph into big voices, big movements, big thoughts. Suddenly you're confronted with how big you really are.

Orange Hand Notes:

In the Circle we connect right hand down, left hand up—it is about giving and receiving.

Use various parts of the body in the warm-up. Encourage multi-levels; up on tip toes and down close to the floor. Encourage use of the whole body. Face different directions. Demonstrate.

Announce that you will be making gentle adjustments to the body so that people can anticipate being touched. Theater is physical and playful and close. Bodies communicate.

Week Three...

storytelling is introduced along with script development. Each week a pair of facilitators conducts the warm-ups and games. This week we begin the book seminar presentations with Liz Lerman's *Critical Response Process*. Her book outlines one of my favorite techniques for maintaining a safe atmosphere and encouraging honest feedback for creative work in the studio.

Orange Hand Notes:
The difference between self-consciousness and self-awareness is judgment.
Making a sound about how you feel is an ongoing practice, we introduce it at the top and continue throughout the work. It is a basic, primal, and immediate way to identify where you are and where you are not.

Every Monday at five p.m. we eat dinner together as a company. We work from six to ten p.m. Facilitators have to come in early to set up and stay late to clean up. You can see it is more demanding than most had been exposed to, though in my mind it is only the start of the level I expect them to achieve. Very soon it is clear who will be strong enough to facilitate for corporate clients, a handful out of the sixteen will be ready after this initial four-month training. Predictably people drop out when they see that beyond the fun of Brown Paper, the rigor of facilitation is not for them.

Weeks Four and Five...
"Viewpoints" is an innovative process for developing performance ensemble, sharpening improvisation, and establishing a shared physical language for production. It was created by choreographer Mary Overlie

and adapted for actors by directors Anne Bogart and Tina Landau. As we go deep into this practice, it starkly reveals where participants are hiding from observers and from themselves. On the "grid" as we call it, you are exposed.

Orange Hand Notes:
Music is vital to the studio. Music either reinforces or changes the mood as your direction requires.

Ideas come from the entire body, we want to wake up and engage the whole person and remove barriers to communication.

People respond because they're looking for this, looking for something new, something to shake up the redundancy of their lives.

You go to Brown Paper Studio because you want more of yourself.

You are courageous enough to want to offer others more of themselves as well.

Weeks Six and Seven...
we've hit our stride by now, we've got warm-ups and games and storytelling and Viewpoints, and the first glimmer of a script is peeking through. We discuss two books by two great directors, *The Empty Space* by Peter Brook and *A Sense of Direction* by William Ball. Brook gives theater context in society. Ball reminds us of our responsibility to beauty.

Orange Hand Notes:
Notice the difference in your life when you're using the tools and when you stop—when you fall off of your own disciplined practice. Get to know yourself by having a practice: yoga, sports, arts, crafts—anything where you will show up regularly and be responsible to yourself and ultimately to others.

One never knows who will stay and who will go. Not everyone wants change, and not everyone will embrace the new; those who do will see you and will stay. It's not personal.

Week Eight...

we are scheduled to experiment with facilitating "Difficult Conversations." I eat some tainted fish on Sunday afternoon at the Waterfront, get food poisoning, and am too sick for Monday's session. In six years directing Brown Paper Studio, I have rarely missed teaching for any reason, and ironically my absence for this particular topic foreshadows what will be our dissolution as a partnership—an inability to have difficult conversations.

Orange Hand Notes:
Trusting yourself means trusting that you are enough.
You are good enough, smart enough, attractive enough, confident enough, humble enough, clear enough, honest enough.
Just because you're you, you get to live the life you deserve.

Weeks Nine and Ten...

We investigate Augusto Boal's Theatre of the Oppressed, explore Keith Johnstone's classic *Impro*, do a quick survey of Applied Theater history. All of it is just the beginning of what one needs to qualify for this work.

Our script has a title, *Out There!*, and is taking shape to premiere on May 25 for an invited audience of corporate guests. Earlier that same day we are sharing our space with Badilisha Poetry X-Change in celebration of Africa Day, the international commemoration of the Organization for African Unity's founding in 1963. The synchronicity of dates for this collaboration feels auspicious.

Orange Hand Notes:

"Being on" means being conscious. You are always on when facilitating, aware of your own breath, listening closely, feeling the impulses of your body, speaking with integrity, having patience, perseverance, and a sense of humor.

This is what is required of the performer. It is not so much putting on a face, as most people assume before they have any experience in the performing arts. It is about allowing your own face to emerge.

You will discover that you have many faces, many personas.

All are to be honored.

There is an exercise called "Homage to Magritte", for me, it will always be "Verna's Belt." Several everyday items are placed on the floor, allowing the actor to choose one. In the space of a few minutes, she or he must use the item in a variety of ways other than its design: a hat could become a pillow, a breast, a kite, a sandwich—whatever comes to mind. The idea is to move the ideas along rapidly, to get out of one's way, to break through the editing mind. Verna, who is new to Brown Paper Studio and to the arts in general, volunteers and chooses a brown leather belt. Right away she discovers a few things: a jump rope, a tail, a bracelet. Then she becomes stuck, completely stumped, and looks out at us helplessly for most of the next few minutes. I coach gently,

"Keep going...let the ideas flow...play with it." Her facial expression becomes even more exasperated. Finally her time is up. We applaud as we always do, because just getting up there and putting yourself on the spot deserves praise. I know she's had a rough time.

"How was it?"

"I couldn't think of anything...I mean, I had ideas, but they seemed too..."

"Too what?"

"Too heavy, too dark..."

"Like what?"

"Well...okay...I thought of hanging myself with the belt...or maybe using the belt as a weapon to beat someone or to destroy something...or that it was a snake..." She pauses, rattled. "The ideas just got worse..."

"What's wrong with these ideas?" I ask. "They are excellent. They are dark. Creativity comes from the dark. The most beautiful flowers come from underground, from the pitch-black earth. Babies are born sightless from a dark womb. Some of our most moving music comes from the pit of the soul. You frustrated yourself wanting to be nice, acceptable, positive, and in the process, suppressed your truly creative urges. We could see you struggling to keep down these powerful, dramatic images. We have to embrace the shadow to make it through to the light. It is the story of being alive, and we owe ourselves our own truths, no matter how messy or raw. Think of how many times a day we sit on our truth and at the same time squash our creative genius. Dare to trust your shadow." Verna is tearful and relieved. Someone hugs her when she comes back to the audience. She provides a great teaching for us all.

Orange Hand Notes:

This work is not therapy. Although it may be therapeutic, this is theater.

Brown Paper requires an emotional and physical fitness. Use the discipline of your

creative training. We want to be able to hold more charge, more life force, and our

bodies are vehicles that need to be nourished, rested, open.

Stuff will come up and it's all yours. Honor the dark. Embrace it.

At home in New York, family matters are pressing. I know I won't
be able to stay here much longer, and I have to come to terms with the
fact that I'll be leaving South Africa before this intensive is complete.
Salim's experience working with me in theatre plus his fundamental
respect for artists makes him the best choice to take over for me on this
new show. He's been hearing my words literally since the womb. I opened
The Death of Black & White nine days before he was born. Commitment
to the ensemble is his mother's milk. When I leave Cape Town my son
becomes the director.

Orange Hand Notes:

We are saying much more with our bodies and our tone of voice than we do with

language. How wonderful then to be able to say exactly what you want with your

entire being, to be in alignment, body, mind, and psyche.

Practice making peace with yourself about yourself.

My last Brown Paper Studio workshop in South Africa is in Polok-
wane, a city north of Johannesburg close to the Zimbabwean border.
Salim and I are facilitating as part of a team led by the business consultancy's founding director. We are contracted to work with sixty

treasury department personnel over two days. By phone and by e-mail, the director and I, assisted by her three top-notch colleagues, organize a combination of games, creativity exercises, and meditations to complement the government agency's strategic-planning sessions. It is the largest group I have ever facilitated, plus it is all adults who are accountants, administrators, and finance professionals. These are heavy-duty left-brainers.

Our facilitation team convenes over a cordial dinner at a seafood restaurant; the six of us get acquainted and strategize our two days together. With a healthy dose of improvisation, we execute seamlessly; no one would know we'd just met hours before. What we exhibit is a fine example of synergy between art and business. Despite my growing skepticism about one-off engagements back in Cape Town, I give a sincerely glowing presentation to the directors and the intensive trainees. After the high of our success, it becomes clear it's time to get on a plane; I cannot be away from my mother any longer. She urgently needs her daughter home full-time.

Leaving South Africa means Medi and I will be that much farther away from each other. My dedication to this long-distance relationship baffles me. Other than Brown Paper Studio, he who lives so tenuously has been the most constant element in my life. He restored my confidence in myself as a woman. I never believed him when he assured me at the beginning, "Judyie, we will be together for years and years."

Through it all, Medi delivered pizza, peddled vacuum cleaners door-to-door, hustled soccer boots and T-shirts from the trunk of the car, worked construction sites, shot pool for bets, translated court cases for bewildered refugees who spoke only Swahili or Lingala, was a print model for sportswear, drove a makeshift taxi, started a soccer team, lost it and started one again, organized tournaments, supported his sister, and periodically gave his clothes and money away to the poor, then came to me for more clothes and money. His poverty made me angry. His generosity made me proud. Even when I know the deck is stacked, I blame him for being on the bottom, a vicious cycle when the man you love exists in the margins on the outskirts of the edge. I am ashamed at my arrogance. Whatever happens I can always fly away to America, to another life where most people have lots and lots of things, including a U.S. passport.

Through it all, Medi consistently played high-level, fair-minded, uplifting, luminous, passionate football, the Beautiful Game in all its glory—win, lose, or draw.

Through it all, he has himself.

On the agency website, Brown Paper Studio was promoted as "Not for the faint-hearted." How true. There is always a time during production when you say, "I want to give up, it's a mess, this will never work, I'm going to embarrass myself," and that's exactly the time when you press on. It's part of the process, and when it appears you know, "There it is, there's the shadow, there's the shit, there's Verna's Belt," and you work through it by showing up, by breathing, by being honest, by communicating. There is always a moment of doubt or fear or insecurity in any show, the unknown lurks in any creative endeavor. A professional artist knows that the shadow, the scary part, the fear of failure, is your friend because it's the one that will lead you to the next level. In theater we get to face the demons together, in a ritual way, as individuals and as the collective, and that's exactly why the process is so potent. It is not for the faint-hearted.

Out There! is written just like every other devised theater script since *D'CIPHER: Set the Record Round.* Before I leave, we start with exercises and discussion to get a sense of what we want to say. We are building a show for business people, so we create writing prompts about the workplace. The material consists of short scenes and monologues; it is compelling, funny, and theatrical. As the long-distance dramaturg, I e-mail the first draft back to Cape Town by mid-April and even with a reasonable five weeks to mount a show it is more than difficult maintaining a consistent rehearsal period given the divergent schedules of professionals and students. Time crunch becomes serious and Salim's task as director is brutal. The company has to rehearse the show in pieces, unable to have coherent run-throughs. Some of our performers are making their stage debuts; simply memorizing lines is daunting. The natural anxiety of performing is exacerbated by the pressure of time. Two weeks before the show, a longtime company member quits the show, complaining about the lack of rehearsal. Salim and I cast an understudy, and he is brought up to speed. Tensions are mounting—made worse without proper communication. The difficult conversations do not happen and therein lies the rub that spells the end of our art and business collaboration. Ours was a great experiment while it lasted, an exhilarating time that ends badly. It will be among the most valuable lessons of all.

Out There! opens to an empty house. No audience. Management says that it was due to the inconvenient time, during lunch hour, and the invited guests were unable to stay for the show. My son says that the sparse audience was escorted out to attend a meeting rather than see the show that was deemed unacceptable. The incident is a glaring example of the ambiguity that characterized too many of our interactions; any confidence in the partnership is destroyed.

There were ways we could have weathered the storm. The opening could have been postponed and more fully rehearsed, or performed as an open studio rehearsal with a talkback following. As an arts company and business consultants, we did not have a shared vocabulary of success. There was not enough trust to say, "We've got a problem, what needs to be done, how do we work this out together?" Hindsight is twenty-twenty.

Our "product" was not a sequence of theater games and creativity techniques; those can be read in a book. Our real product is the ability to create ensemble, and the bond within a performing arts company must be respected. We ask people to put their vulnerable, creative selves onstage, and saying "you're not good enough" is not an option.

If we had made it past the dragon's mouth of *Out There!*, we would truly have created a product, something the world is looking for and will pay for, a sense of belonging, a sense of community and mutual trust. You have to stand together until the final bow. My dear Miki was there to midwife the cast, her arms open to catch the baby, to applaud to say, 'Good job because you worked past the fear'. "Mom," my son tells me, "Miki was there for us." That knowledge of how to stay the course is part of what makes an artist, and as devastating as it was to Salim, he made it. True to his lineage, he is backstage to greet his cast at the curtain call. Ultimately that's who we are—Brown Paper Studio is an artistic family through good times and bad. This last show is strangely perfect with its vacant seats and cold Cape Town winter weather. It is the end of an era.

Flying home to New York, Salim makes a connection in Dubai and accidently leaves his production journal on the plane. It is no mistake. He doesn't want to be reminded of the pain. He has been initiated into the theater. He has his own war story, and he has earned his stripes.

In the following weeks I schedule staff meetings via Skype that rarely happen and my regularly requested conference calls dwindle to none. I'm informed of the office and studio's actual closure date after the fact. To their credit my business partners continue to deposit funds in my South African bank account over the next few months, adequate financial restitution for the tremendous work accomplished. Disappointment at the demise of our studio and our failed association is overshadowed when an ambulance takes my mother to the emergency room one Saturday morning in October. A CT-scan reveals a mass on her lung. All the hollow mornings of "I want my mother" stab me again. Our family will be in denial for weeks, imagining that it's not really cancer, not really malignant, not really deadly. It's what one has to do when another world is about to collapse.

ॐ

2010

Love
Light

I remember. . .I remember.

It will take me a month before I can say the words "my mother died." When I finally speak them, it will sound like they come from someone else's mouth.

None of that has happened yet when I contact my faithful company members:

Dear Brown Paper,

It's been awhile since I've written this special salutation that was my compass for so many years. I never imagined I would be away this long. I miss you all so much and even though we are separated by time and space, every day I am grateful for my life in Cape Town. It's been a challenging year since I saw you last. Most significantly, my lively spirited 93-year-old mother that some of you met when she visited in 2006 was diagnosed with cancer in October. As her primary caregiver, my life has taken on a different shape and rhythm. I am deeply grateful for the opportunity to care for my mother—I understand now why I had to return to the States.

Employment here is sporadic at best. For the past few weeks I was part of a visual/performing arts ensemble at one of New York's major museums, and currently I am a census worker, meaning I walk door-to-door with an official U.S. government badge asking questions about how many people live in house, how old are they, etc. It's sho'nuff grunt work. Although I've never worked for the Feds I feel okay about it because Obama is President—plus I get a check. Through it all I have been writing about Brown Paper Studio, about how despite all the insanity in both of our countries, we are determined to usher in this new world, a world where creativity, kindness, generosity, integrity, mutuality, joy, fairness, and love, always love, are honored. Never forget that this is what we stand for, even if we forget and falter and fall, we get up and go on. Be gentle with yourselves, show yourselves the compassion that you wish to see in others because surely we are change agents. Consider yourselves pioneers. . .

Days before Thanksgiving we receive mother's biopsy test results. Her illness draws Shahid back into my life, into all of our lives. He has plans to drive north with his partner to celebrate the holiday at her sister's house. He comes to visit for the afternoon and ends up staying till the next day, up until five in the morning finishing a bottle of Jameson Irish Whiskey with the kids and talking. Our Kentucky side of the family is famous for this particular style of all-night life, we cook and drink and tell stories and watch movies and relax together until the wee hours. Shahid's wisdom and experience is such that when he is present, a room shapes itself around him. His gray beard and long dreads attest to the time it has taken to achieve this stature. He was the primary caregiver for his mother, brother, and father—all dying from cancer in a span of two years. He is the veteran of a grim battlefront. He counsels us, "You have to just sit there. Be with them. Don't think about the end—think about today. You have today." He tells us he slept in a chair next to each of his loved ones' beds. He carried them in his arms when they were too weak to walk. We listen with reverence and with apprehension because his voice is husky with memories as he describes the details of death.

I remember. . .the ragged smell of salt air rising off Cape Town harbor. . .

I remember. . .being flattered more than once, when a South African person said to me, "You are South African, you are home". . .

I remember. . .driving into Prince Albert, turning out the headlights, getting out of the truck to look at the stars. . .stars that reach down to the horizon. . .I gaze in awe on this empty midnight road at the bottom of Africa. . .I thought stars like this were just something a schoolgirl sees on a field trip to the planetarium, something only pretend. . .

I remember almost being deported because I was too lazy or too arrogant or both to renew my visa. . .

I remember greeting people on the street, in the shops, at work, and asking them about their family before discussing business. . .

I remember. . .talking fast on the phone because the airtime was about to run out. . .sending a proudly South African "please call me" because the airtime did run out. . .

I remember...shouts of our Glendale company when we arrived for Brown Paper Studio after school... "They are here! They are here!"...

I remember Sunday walks along Seapoint with my closest and most compassionate confidante, the ocean...

I remember, I remember...

Soon after Christmas and the New Year, it becomes clear that my mother is gravely ill. I ask her if she wants to live. "Oh yes," she replies in earnest. "I love life. I want to be here as long as I can. I just don't know if my body will last." I sit on the floor in front of her La-Z-Boy recliner, my tear-stained face in her lap. "Please, Mommy," I plead, "give us more time. Please don't leave. Not yet." She steadies my shaking shoulders. "I'll stay as long as I can. I promise I will." By sheer force of will, she does stay, enduring the burden of an oxygen machine, debilitating treatments, vomiting, dehydration, locked bowels, no appetite, no energy, no strength. She graciously gives us all a chance to make peace with the prospect of losing her.

In February, Mother must undergo radiation to relieve excruciating back pain. Her tumors are spreading. I have found temporary work at the Guggenheim Museum. I haven't earned any money for months. I can't take her to the clinic every day and work, even part-time. I need help. I call Shahid.

"When do you want me to come?" is his response, and like the man he has always been and will always be, he arrives three weeks later. Exactly as he prescribed, he just sits with Mommy, eases her fear, nausea, and exhaustion with his comforting presence. Together they watch her favorite contentious political talk shows, along with her daily dose of droning congressional hearings. Like old times, they discuss current events; she poses incisive questions and marvels at his unflinching analysis. Her memory is slipping, and he, patient with the repetitions of the elderly, doesn't mind holding the same conversations with her every day. After being absent for a decade, he is back home. He is her son, again. We are a family, again. In the midst of unbearable loss, we mend. In the tumultuous years since Shahid and I have called each other husband and wife, our love for each other has done the only thing that true love can ever do, and that is to grow.

Dear Brown Paper,

Hanan and Salim are doing okay given the difficult circumstances. Via Facebook you might know more about the details of their lives than I do. It is a gift to be all together at this time of their grandmother's passing. Africa taught me about family, and you are all my art family. We will teach the world what that means.

I'm watching the buildup to World Cup in disbelief that I'm not there and with a sense of pride that I personally know South Africa and her people. I started buying lottery tickets with a plan to hop on a plane for even two weeks so I can be in the Mother City when the new stadium roars as the whole world watches. Who knows? If any of you dream lucky numbers please send them to me. It's certainly no more of a far-fetched way to raise money than writing grant proposals.

Medi and I are still in contact, we talk as often as we can, mostly shouting on poor phone connections that last only a few expensive minutes. These absurd conversations keep my heart open, I'm confident we'll be together again. That's true for all of us, because nothing can stop the force of love, and that, My Darlings, is what I feel for each of you...

While caring for Mother during her radiation treatments, Shahid mentions that he's going to the Vineyard in May. She lights up, clapping her hands. "Oh! I would love to see the Island in spring." He agrees to take her with him, and in doing so grants what will turn out to be her most ardent dying wish. Financially our family is no longer living on fumes, we are living on ether. Somehow we purchase a plane ticket to bring Shahid back, rent a car, and delicately pack pillows around Mother in the front seat to send her off for her last holiday. The night before she leaves, she's wearing her little white Keds sneakers and tapping her cane next to her suitcase, an eager summer camper ready for the morning bus. "I am such a fortunate woman. I get to see the Island one last time."

Ten days into her visit, mother's body begins its final descent. Her internal bleeding is so severe she must be flown via helicopter to Boston in the middle of the night. The next morning, arriving at Massachusetts General, I am greeted by two very serious, very young emergency-room doctors. They question me about the particulars of the "do not resuscitate" orders and exactly how aggressive do I want to be in regard to prolonging my elderly mother's life. I tell them I must see her first. When I grasp her hand it's as delicate as tissue paper. "Judyie," she says smiling, "in my whole life I've never been in a helicopter before, the sky was so blue and the sun was so bright. It was fun. It was really cool."

For a week Mother and I are alone in Boston, it is our oasis. She charms everyone at Mass General, nurses, doctors, physical therapists, cleaning staff, and social workers. As Shahid had instructed me what seems like eons ago, I sleep in a chair next to her bed. Her caregivers recognize these are days we will never have again and bring a cot for me to sleep on, essentially giving us a private room. In our sterile, white sanctuary, we say "I love you" often. We doze holding hands. We do not talk about dying; the closest I can get is to whisper, "Mommy, will you stay close, no matter what?" "Of course, Jude, I'll always be with you." When she naps, I leave the hospital to care for myself, wandering Beacon Hill at sunset lost in the architecture, or treating myself to a sushi dinner with too much wine, or indulging in a metallic orange and hot pink mani pedi. Constantly she asks me, "Jude, when are we going home?" "Soon, Mommy, soon." After days spent stabilizing her condition with blood transfusions, the doctors advise that she is still too weak to survive a trip back to New York. I protest and am ferocious about the fact that my mother will not die separated from all those who love her. I plot our getaway, planning to rent a comfortable Lincoln Continental car and oxygen tanks, and take a chance driving down the highway. Seeing how serious I am, the hospital makes it possible for an ambulance to transport us. Despite overwhelming odds, she makes it back to a New York hospital, this stalwart soul who, even in the process of dying, was as fully alive as any of us could ever hope to be.

I remember seeing the mountain for the first time, thinking, "I know this place, I have come back"…walking streets where everyone looks like me, skin like me, hair like me…

I remember…countless incredible sunsets from my window…a living, liquid canvas of turquoise, gold, peach, magenta, platinum, crimson, and ash…

I remember…wondering where the money to do anything was going to come from…relief when the money finally appeared…

I remember…the exact corner…the particular phone booth near the fountain in the middle of town where my Internet lover rejected me… how the wind ripped…how my insides collapsed at the disdain in his eyes…

I remember…against all common sense…buying handmade gold and gemstone jewelry on layaway at Shaheen's jewelry shop…

I remember my small, square office in the university's English Department…a hub, a sanctuary, a crossroads for students…

I remember…I thought I would never have to leave for long… knowing someday I would have to leave for who knows how long…

I remember…

🜋

On her first day in home hospice care, Mother asks me, "Am I going to get better?" She sounds like a little girl. I lie to her. I lie to myself. "The doctors have offered their best treatments, and even though they say there is no more they can do, only you can say if you will recover." She says nothing. Just like a little girl, she knows you have not told the whole truth and also knows she's not going to get any more truth out of you.

Mommy slips away amidst our exhaustion, hope, anxiety, laughter and tears. We watch her fade; losing memory and weight, becoming more transparent, more luminous, more loving. Her vomit and bowels are dark with blood. She can only suck on ice chips or mange dribbles of ginger ale onto her tongue. Reduced to wearing diapers and rolled over side to side like meat to keep from developing bedsores, she barely complains. As she is turned and washed and changed like a baby, rather than being humiliated, she remarks how good it feels to be so carefully tended. She manages to find a silver lining even as an invalid.

"One more day," our hearts are bleeding, too, "please, one more day." She has nights of delirious conversations with the spirit world. She travels to the Other Side, wrestling her dead sister, the same sister she fought in life. "Let me go, Clara," she protests, "leave me alone." She speaks to my late father, assures him, "I'm coming, George. I'll be there in a minute." Coming out of reverie, she announces to Hanan, "I'm going!"

"Where Grandma? Where are you going?"

Mommy's voice is emphatic. "To heaven!"

I won't ever be able to smell Dolce Gabana's "Light Blue" without evoking the sublime presence of the last hospice nurse. She is a very pretty brown-skinned woman whose delicate perfume fills the bedroom that has become a sickroom. While we finally sleep after our grueling week of hospice care, she strokes Mother's limbs, checks her pulse, stands over her bed in attendance. On manic alert, my restless body is up and down all night, and not once when I pass by the room is the sweetly scented angelic nurse seated.

In death, as in life, Mother is generous to the end. She surrenders her last breath to one of her adopted daughters, who knows that being the one present at this final moment is a testament of love. I am in the next room figuring out how to schedule another surreal day of home hospice care. When I see her stone-still and slack-jawed in the bed, I believe it and I don't. It happened and it couldn't. After so many months of coming to her bedroom at night to confirm that her chest was rising and falling, the way a new mother compulsively checks the crib to make sure her infant is alive, I stand still and stare a long time, sure Mommy's chest will rise again. She dies on Memorial Day weekend, on a sparkling late spring day that radiates all the promise of summer. She lets go when she knows we could handle it on our own—even if we don't think so. As we walk along the Hudson, holding each other up, she seems to be everywhere, suspended in the diamond-studded atmosphere itself.

I remember...people speaking to me in Afrikaans...the look of surprise at my American accent, "Sorry, I speak only English"...

I remember...being dispirited and disgusted at being ignored and marginalized and trivialized and patronized...losing faith and hope and patience...crying all alone in my apartment because I knew what I was doing...I knew it was important...I knew someday it would be recognized...

I remember...the warm, shallow surf at Muizenberg...children playing in the waves...the beach filled with whole families of many colors...

I remember...the Waterfront choked with tourists who shop all day in air conditioning, snap lots of photos, ride antiseptic buses, and swear they've been to Africa...

I remember...cozy around the fire at our theater camp... telling stories of ourselves that can only be shared in flickering shadow and light...

I remember…hiking the mountains, humbled by the beauty…staring long and hard, then closing my eyes to tattoo the view strong on my skin…sure that in the ice and cement of North America, I will need these full-body memories…

I remember I remember I remember I remember…

My mother's funeral is in June on the opening day of the Soccer World Cup in South Africa. After the ceremony at my brother's church around the corner from our apartment, I come home and sit in her easy chair to see the first matches. I think about how she and I planned to watch the games together. I refused to wear black to the service. I'm wearing a white linen summer dress and drinking white sparkling wine. All around me the house is filled with people. No one brings any food, so we have to send out for pizza. This makes me sad, because in her life my mother fed so many people. On Monday, my children, Shahid, my brother, and I will take her ashes way out on Long Island to a military cemetery to rest alongside my ex-Marine father's ashes. Today there is nothing more to do than watch South Africa shine for the whole world.

To my bewildered heart, my mother is not dead. She's just not here. Because she is always happy to see me when I enter her bedroom, I expect to see her turn to greet me, I expect to hear "Hey Jude!" with unwavering enthusiasm in her warm, welcoming contralto. No matter how many times I go into her room, she's not here. Where is she?

By some bizarre irony, in August I get work as an office temp at a cemetery. I need the money. I sit at a computer doing data entry on a backlog of burial information. I have to confirm that the dead people listed on index cards are properly logged into the system as being either in an urn, a crypt, or a grave. I consider this cruel. I wonder why the Universe has such a sick sense of humor. Toward the end of the second day of sitting for eight hours doing a kind of reverse census work, I frantically text my daughter, "I'm getting the hell out of here….no pun intended." She firmly talks me off the ledge, "It's for one week, take a walk and calm down."

August brings the legendary dog days of summer, yet we New Yorkers behave more like sheep, bleating constantly about the heat. "How Hot It Is," the inescapable conversation. When I go for a walk at lunchtime, my office mates remind me, "It's really hot today…like ninety-eight degrees or something."

"Yeah, I know, I just need to get out for a bit," and proceed through the door. What I don't tell them is if I stay inside, I'll start screaming and rolling on the floor and pulling out my Afro, and then it will be even hotter.

The air in the hundred-year-old cemetery does not move. Even insects don't bother to fly. I walk among old and new gravestones beneath a massive cathedral of sycamore trees. The trees talk to me, tell me they have witnessed generations of people in extreme stages of grief. The trees tell me their arms were wide enough to hold them all, and they promise me, we can hold you too.

While I walk, I make up stories about the dead. From their names and the years they were born and died and the style and inscriptions and sometimes pictures on their tombstone, I imagine their lives and dramas. I wonder if someone still loves them, still misses them. From my fantasies I realize how important it is to find the dead when the living come paying homage. I become very careful with the mindless task of data entry. I don't want anyone to be misplaced or overlooked. I don't want someone to search for their mother and she can't be found.

On Friday I reach into my closet and pull out the white dress I wore to the funeral. I thought it would take me a year, if ever, to put it back on. "Forget it," Hanan warns me when I suggest the linen outfit looks like a cool choice. I want to wear it on my last day at work in the old graveyard next to the Long Island Expressway. The cemetery stands its silent vigil, ignored alongside a major roadway filled with very alive people whizzing by on their way to the airports before going on to everywhere else. Today is an absolute oven, the grass is more brown than green, you can feel the trees aching their roots down one more inch for water. As I walk in the uncompromising heat, I intuit, quite unexpectedly, that these trees and cobblestones and graves have healed the first thin onionskin layer of the wound that is my mother's death. She is not here. Not anymore. Where is she? In the privacy of the parched afternoon, I weep for her and for myself, because I know that just as I was once inside my mother, she is now inside of me.

I remember. . .driving into the sheer depths of the Karoo's Die Hel valley. . . gazing in awe at the cave paintings in the Cedarburg. . .choosing handmade shoes to buy in Wippertal. . .cheering for the whales in Hermanus. . .

I remember. . .riding third class on the train, packed and sweaty and smelly. . .grateful for a seat to savor my bag of sweet and chewy Maynard's Jelly Baby candies. . .

I remember...all the patient people who helped me with multiple forms and licenses and applications...their amusement at my nonstop persistence...day after day of wearing down the pavement in cheap flip-flops...one tired foot in front of the other, dogged and determined to live this unconventional, improvisational life...

I remember...hanging clean sheets in the fresh air with wooden clothespins...black crow with a white stripe in a blue sky sails overhead...

I remember...each one of our Brown Paper Studios, spacious rooms with windows and light...first UWC, then Azaad, on Harrington Street...always thinking, "This is it, we are finally home"...having to leave them all...

I remember...sitting on a bench in the Company's Gardens surrounded by trees and rosebushes, a bamboo grove and every color flower blooming...the sun full on my face...amazed that despite it all, I am still in Cape Town.

"Now that Mom is gone, you and Hanan, you must love each other more," Medi's voice consoles me. There is some irony in calling from Manhattan to Lubumbashi in the Democratic Republic of Congo for comfort. I dial from the one of the richest nations on earth to a war zone to fortify my heart. Such is the true resourcefulness of Africa. A two-dollar phone card gives Medi and me seven static-filled minutes, abysmally poor reception, a time-delayed audio so we're constantly

talking over each other. "Say it again…I'll be quiet now…you talk…
what?…no, you first…okay…what?…say it again…no, you first…I'll speak
now…" While he cooks his dinner of rice, milk, and sugar, I get the
soccer report. "We played today, we lost two to one. I scored the only
goal. Yesterday, we won four to two. I scored two goals." He manages
to score goals on rice, milk, and sugar, using every remaining ounce of
energy to find more rice and milk and sugar to live another day. All
too quickly the recorded announcement comes on, saying, "You have
one minute remaining." Before our money runs out, his voice cheers
me. "Don't worry, Judyie, don't worry. The time will come; we will be
together. I am there with you always. My spirit is there with you." Then
it's time to say good-bye, to make kissing and hugging sounds, to say, "I
love you very much, take…" The last words "…care of yourself" are lost
under the automated voice, "Your call has been terminated because you
no longer have sufficient funds." Like we need to be reminded.

When Medi and I lived on the beach in that charming apartment with
the picture-postcard view of Table Mountain, he told me how it would
happen. "Judyie, you will write my story." The tone in his voice sounded
like I'd just won the lottery—it's been decided, I am his biographer. My
first response was to roll my eyes. "Yeah, right." Then I wondered if it's
true, will I write the story of this marvelous man who epitomizes Africa?
His valiant tale is one among the millions of valiant tales that together
manifest the genius of the Continent. His portrait is one in an unbroken
legacy of self-determination. African people's brilliance, achievement,
ingenuity, fortitude, creativity, and faith are transcendent. The cradle of
humanity remains the foundation for humanity's continued evolution.

Dear Brown Paper,

It's time to write our how-to manual about Brown Paper Studio. It's time to gather together to document our experience; how we changed ourselves, our communities, and our world.

I spoke at an arts education conference recently about how we transcended divisions and separations within a society with creativity—the world is hungry for who we are and what we've done. Brown paper, colored markers, music, fruit, and Love—our recipe for Transformation.

Living on a new earth, the conversation is no longer east and west, male and female, rich and poor, black and white. *Those were the old days.* We're integrating the right- and left-brain functions, connecting the head and the heart, bringing the creative and linear into the unity that evolution has promised us from the beginning. After standing up on two legs eons ago, the new human being is finally taking our next step, spreading our wings, and flying into our rightful heritage as divine. As we let go of thinking too much and trust the feeling, we ascend. In life, as in Medi's fundamental football philosophy, one has to learn how to get out of one's own way. It is a game. You must always remember to play.

These are the New Days.

꙳

Epilogue

Once upon a time
in a time that is now
She came to Earth
in the beginning
so there could be a Beginning

She forgot who she was and
in her forgetting
Time began

this is the story of how she remembered
this is the story
of the End of Time

She wanted to find her Great Love and
what she had to learn is
She is Her Great Love

it is the happiest of endings
that never ends...

> brown paper, #22 Montreux
> Cape Town, South Africa
> February 2003

Made in the USA
Lexington, KY
15 January 2013